How to Write Poetry in How Many Chapters

Also by Maurice Whelan and published by Ginninderra Press
Boat People
The Lilac Bow
Excalibur's Return
A Season and a Time
Spirit Eyes
Thought: The Invisible Essence

Maurice Whelan

How to Write Poetry in How Many Chapters

Acknowledgements

My thanks to Michael Dudley, Winton Higgins, Catherine Hickie, Tom Ilbery and Elaine Kelly

My continuing thanks to Stephen Matthews for publishing my work

How to Write Poetry in How Many Chapters
ISBN 978 1 76109 485 9
Copyright © text Maurice Whelan 2023
Cover image: Shahid Najeeb

First published 2023 by
Ginninderra Press
PO Box 3461 Port Adelaide 5015
www.ginninderrapress.com.au

Contents

Preface	9
1. Making a Poem: A Brief Outline	11
2. Making a Poem: A Detailed Account	12
3. The Resplendent Fabric of the Universe	18
4. Poetry in a Time of Pandemic	46
5. Loving Words	74
6. Beginnings	78
7. The Enchanter's Cell	85
8. Poems as Dreams and Dreams as Poems	89
9. Ars Poetica	91
10. Might Half-slumbering	92
11. An Invisible Hand	95

The poem is an attempt at self-recovery, self-recognition, self-remembering, the marvel of being again. That this happens at times, happens in poems in many different and contradictory ways, is as great a mystery as the mystery of being itself and cause for serious thought.

                                                                    Charles Simic

What we call meaning, what we call resonance, enchantment, and ultimately beauty, would remain totally unfathomed and silent without art. Art is the agent. Art allows us to reach our truest, deepest, most enduring selves by borrowing someone else's skill, someone else's words, or someone else's gaze and colours; left to our own devices, we wouldn't have the insight, or the comprehensive vision, much less the will or the courage, to enter that place where only art can take us.

                                                                    Andre Aciman

Preface

This is a story about poetry. There is a large story. Inside the large story there is a small story. The large story is about how poems are written. I select poems from my four books of poetry and some as yet unpublished and describe what went into their writing. I use themes and headings to give some order to the poems.

The small story is about Covid-19. In late 2019, news came out of China that a virus had broken the barrier between animals and humans. A wet market in Wuhan was identified as the origin of what became known as the coronavirus or Covid-19. The epidemic became a pandemic. Throughout 2020 and 2021, it spread to all corners of the globe, killed millions, infected hundreds of millions and triggered social and economic crises.

As the world was turned upside down by the pandemic, I became aware, in retrospect, that I had responded to my upside-downness with poetry. I had written more poems than in any similar time frame. It wasn't planned, but the poems had a sequential pattern and were an intuitive response to the changing circumstances in the world. And Covid-19 remains with us, so it, and efforts to think about it, continue.

When I return to the larger story of writing poetry, I extend my exploration of it. It is one thing to get started as a writer. It is another to sustain a creative writing life. I select a few poets who have written about how they established, defined and sustained themselves. There is an exploration of the relationship between dreams and poetry, of language and the benefits of knowing the way language has shaped who we are and how a love of words is essential if you are to become a poet.

And a rather simple question is posed: what is poetry? Is its essence definable or is it like other forms of art forever elusive?

How To Write Poetry In How Many Chapters is a companion piece to my recently published book *Thought: The Invisible Essence*, in which poetry played a significant if supporting role to the prose text. Here we have reversal: the poet-writer becomes the main character. Prose is prologue, epiloge, director and stage manager, all constructing a space where the poetic voice can speak and be listened for.

1
Making a Poem: A Brief Outline

1. Some sensory experience, a word or a phrase makes an impression. I sense the possibility of a poem. No ordered thinking of a rational nature is operating.

2. I write some words down on a piece of paper with a pencil or pen.

3. The words begin to grow. The piece skids, gets traction. It feels as if I am going somewhere. Or the whole thing blows up, evaporates and disappears. You come back to words on a page and the spirit that hovered above has departed. Leave it.

4. Or the outline of an idea emerges. There is something important to articulate.

5. The idea becomes firm, solid. Making the poem is now a possibility. Maybe a necessity.

6. The language gains confidence. Words step up. They 'know' what they need to carry.

7. Words take delight in their freshness and newness. They become brave enough to skip and dance. You play like a child. You are as daring as a trapeze artist.

8. The 'construction' is on the flat. I hold my breath as it is about to take flight.

9. The poem circles. The work is done. Anticipation of joy as others raise their eyes to read in the skies.

2
Making a Poem: A Detailed Account

Having briefly described what happens in nine steps, I now go back to each of them to enlarge and elaborate. I explain more about the activity within me as thinking and writing progresses. I'm taking it beyond simply saying a poem makes space or establishes an oasis. Sometimes, a more complete understanding/explanation is revealed through an examination of the details.

1. A significant degree of chaos must be tolerated, even welcomed during the first four steps. A stance of passive, feminine receptivity is best; active, masculine grasping worst. The first impression comes from inside or outside me. Inside origins can be a memory, dream or bodily sensation. From outside: while reading or listening, a phrase, idea, smell, touch, sound, taste. Doing a practical task. Reading a book about anything of interest.

I spend useful time in the pre-literate worlds. They include Homer and pre-Homer times. 'His' – he was most likely a collective – era was one where literature was solely the spoken word. Studying the pre-Homeric Greek poets, for example, of whom only scant fragments remain, takes us back to cuneiform and runic scripts.

At the very beginning of a (possible) poem, I am often transported back to ancient Greece, indeed to any pre-literate, pre-alphabetic culture. I can be one of them. I imagine living then, making poetry with no conception that it would ever be written down. There was no such thing as writing.

Before alphabets and writing were invented, music was on the scene. The Greeks played the lyre while poems and stories were spoken. Hence 'lyric poetry'. The music was not simply background entertainment.

Musical language, like visual language, assists the speaker in remembering lines, and enables the listener to see and recall, which, as the neuroscientist will assert, lay down neural pathways in the brain.

I never push myself forward in time out of those ages. When some words acquire music, I pick up my pen. When Seamus Heaney's wife saw his fingers tapping on the steering wheel, she knew a poem was in the making.

2. The physicality of pen and paper is important to me. I don't carry a notebook as I move around as some writers do, although at home and at work there is often one at hand. I find a notebook creates expectations. It's important to vegetate. When, not so long ago, letters arrived in envelopes, the latter were put to good use with the origins of many poems imprinted on them. Nowadays, most people feel a similar at-homeness with a keyboard. Do whatever comes natural to you.

3. Heady times. Passive/active. I am writing/saying it. It is also writing/saying itself. I borrow the shoes of a musical composer; the painter's tools of trade; the sculpture's respect for marble. Listener/speaker.

4. The central idea that underpins the work gains shape and strength. The keelson of a boat is solid and straight. The foundation is firm. Test the strength and durability of that thought. Nod to philosophers, mystics, the great spiritual explorers. William Hazlitt (who, though not a poet, spent much time writing within a poetic space) said, 'Many men set their minds on trifles, and have not the compass of soul to take an interest in anything truly great and important beyond forms and minutiae.' Or Louise Glück may come to mind when she described poems as experiments in search of what is true.

Aim big. You have to have something to say and it has to be truly great and important to you. Others may have come at the idea before but you need faith in the authenticity of your poem. It doesn't have to be big in the sense of changing the world and being recognised far and wide. But it has to be big enough to change you and hold the potential to change at least one other.

5. I am now bricklayer, carpenter, architect, engineer, a site manager engaged in a project of great import. I am a child sitting on a floor with building blocks that have an awkward habit of falling over. I am a dreamer.

I have learned to observe and think about dreams. They are an important part of living a life and for me an important part of making poems. I will say more of the subject later.

Between 4 and 5, the form in which the poem is to be written gets decided upon. I use various forms: free verse, sonnet, villanelle, prose poem, haiku or other short forms. If two lines quickly present as a possible chorus, a villanelle could be indicated. An idea that would best be expressed in two phases points to a sonnet. I use rhyme, half-rhyme and unrhymed forms. The inner music of the early words is usually the decider here. And sometimes, when a few words become a few lines, you get pointed in the right direction.

I know the foundations are solid. Occasionally, the poem wants to end itself. I obey. I don't resist. It is suddenly complete. Its brevity is its strength. I will tell the story of some such poems.

6. An auditorium, a stage envisioned. A large public performance. Or a private audience of a small group. Or of one. Here, I proffer advice to myself. Forget the expectant public performance. It will do your head in. You won't write well if you harbour images of large crowds. Write for two people – one other; or just one – yourself.

If I have declared the poem finished and good, and the majority are the result of much labour and patience, I trust it will be there for you. If I have put part of my soul into it. When times are bad, I will turn to it and it will sustain me. Others need to receive it, to sustain them. That won't happen if you don't offer part of your soul to its conception. I have no control over that. Except when I read/speak it in public, I need to deliver it to the best of my ability, give it a spoken-word life. I need to let the poem read me.

7. It, the poem, has a pulse, muscle life. It moves on its own. It follows and runs ahead of me. I learn it by heart, take walks (I used to run), speak it out loud. The body's movement tests the movement of the poem. I listen to what it has to say for itself.

Rote learning repays a hundredfold. I am my own first audience. As our poem begins to take on a separate existence, we can lose ourself in its vicinity. Find ourself again. It can drift around us; make an appearance in a dream, be in our heart as we go to sleep or wake up.

8. This assemblage of words has never existed before. Their weight, lightness, buoyancy, sturdiness is unique. All individual words and punctuation enjoy their place, whether the leading role or as a member of the chorus.

Before the poem is sent in flight, I step back. It's time for the final judgement, for an honest appraisal of the value of my creation. And a writing group allows that activity to continue. Lots of test flights to prove it flies solo. The final release: a loud, delighted YES!

9. Until the next stimulus arrives, the next spark strikes, as a poem maker I am nothing. This is not a superannuated profession. I wait. There are periods of painful waiting, the lack of artistic work a silent loss. If necessary, I remind myself how lucky I am. Gratitude often dispels pain. What has been done is good and my faith remains attached to it. I trust that when my unconscious is ready, I will start anew and meanwhile recall Emily Dickinson: 'Hope is the thing with feathers / That perches in the soul.'

This is one of the great things about writing poetry and by extension all art. We employ the whole of ourselves in its pursuit. That is why it is so deeply satisfying. The resultant exhilaration can catapult you in all directions. If your poem has surpassed intellectual comment and is unique and authentic, it and you are part of that extensive human effort to bear witness to the mystery of life, to articulate its essence.

Although unlikely to have been given the name. the first sound engineers were surely the architects of churches, synagogues and mosques and other buildings of worship. Scientific measuring devices being unavailable, they relied on the human ear, experimented with space. A poet constructs a similar edifice. Through trial and error, echo chambers of the mind are formed. William Hazlitt again: 'The music of the language answers to the music of the mind.'

A few thoughts about what to do with remnants. Unless you entertain fantasies of posthumous fame – the box containing all your manuscripts and rough drafts discovered in the attic of a house you once lived in – now it's time to cull. Those A4 pages on which appeared the first typed version of the poem, now so filled with corrections and changes, pencil and pen marks the colour of rainbows submerging the print in a sea of arrows, circles, squares, words and phrases climbing up the margins, across the top and down the other side, squiggles, scribbles, doodles, hieroglyphics that no Rosetta Stone, no eager PhD student hoping to make an original mark on the literary world could ever hope to decipher.

And a single poem could have many such pages, the transcribing onto the new what has risen up out of the cauldron of the old, always accompanied by a sense of achievement and hope. It is holding up and, like the clay spinning in the potter's hands, taking shape. But when the job is done and the completed poem has liberty to travel beyond the horizon, into the sights of others, cull, and when the next poem beckons, you will have freed your mind to see the next formation gathering.

Maybe some poets put too much into a poem because they fear they may never write another. The fear, as I have noted, is real. Once the finished poem takes flight, you never know if you will start another. The fear can lead to depression, even desolation; having participated in creation, there is no knowing if you will ever play a part again. No consolation is to be found in the discarded fragments, in the drafts. All must be, I think, allowed to return from whence they came, the depths, the unconscious, a place where time makes its own rules. All we can do is wait, hope and listen. And one night, inside a flower, inside a dream, something stirs. We taste, touch, smell, hear or catch sight of a new creation. Now, that moment has an exhilaration all of its own. For me, it has echoes of being handed your newborn child. For you? I'll leave you to imagine.

All this is said to clear the mind; to remove inhibitions to the new. When Seamus Heaney was asked by Denis O'Driscoll if he was like Wordsworth, 'who early in life had an intense experience…about inanimate nature which he spent…his poetical life trying to describe,' Heaney said,

> The early-in-life experience has been central to me all right. But I'd say you aren't so much trying to describe it as trying to locate it. The amount of sensory material stored up or stored down in the brain's and the body's systems is inestimable. It's like a culture at the bottom of a jar, although it doesn't grow, I think, or help anything else to grow unless you find a way to reach it and touch it. But once you do, it's like putting your hand into a nest and finding something beginning to hatch out in your hand.

Letting go allows for new hatching. We need the dark to give our eyes a rest. So much enters the mind visually. Be grateful for the night.

That's the way I think of leftover words. Something else may work for you.

3
The Resplendent Fabric of the Universe

When asked why he always explored small events and the details of individual or family life and why he avoided or ignored big, global issues, John McGahern, the Irish novelist and short story writer, said the local was the universal with the walls removed. Look closely at small, intimate scenes of life and you uncover concerns and struggles of universal significance.

In this chapter, I go local. I select a theme, a heading, take a single or a few poems I have written over the past fifteen years, tease out what is going on inside the poem, engage with detail.

Using a heading is a bit artificial when a number of themes converge on or criss-cross a single poem. But lifting out pieces of a mosaic or selecting a small section of a large canvas has value and can lead to an enrichment of the whole.

'I'

Together Again

If I say I, or me, or mine, I wish, I want, I will, I won't,
I think, I feel, or I say once upon a time I did this or that,
Take heed. Because an I is prone to wander into another
I, and become if truth be told alike to you.
And following in your shadow – be you old or child,
Tame or wild – bending to your line of light
The poet begins to carve, to chisel, to polish words,
That move and breathe. And when the poem
Is done and serves your I as mirror, I beg pardon,
Must dispose of ye, to backward glance,
On second sights to see those hidden parts of me.

The poet who serves his apprenticeship in the art and craft of poetry graduates with a great honour and a greater responsibility. Both the honour and the responsibility are contained in one word; in a single letter, 'I'. The freedom within poetic form allows expression, permits the many parts that make up the individual 'I', to find their voice. The responsibility on the other hand requires that he lend his 'I' to other 'I's, that, having entered through sympathetic identification with others, speaks on their behalf. And there is more. Where no 'I' is possible, he needs invent one, because the mute seas and skies, flowers and trees, the animals and the birds must have a voice.

> Heaven does with us as we with torches do
> Not light them for ourselves. For if our virtues
> Did not go forth from us, 'twere all alike
> As if we had them not.
>
> *Measure for Measure*

We may be able to judge whether a poet has passed their apprenticeship by his use of 'I'. If it is used to hold a torch to himself, he should go back to school. But if his use of 'I' is expansive and generous, and others are easily able to step inside the poem, search for themselves, virtue will have gone forth and been used as torch for others.

There is no 'I' without 'we'. Each of us began life in the body of another. Separateness conceived as complete separation is a dangerous myth. We move from immature childhood dependency to adult mature dependency. Without others we are starved of what they offer us. And we never learn to give or receive love. The accomplishment of loving another is one of the highest human achievements. In writing, to lend our 'I' to others is, at its best, an act of love. The 'I' the poet uses has lived within the 'I' of others. He can identify with, speak for, be, another 'I'. That is how the torch is used for others.

> The lunatic, the lover and the poet
> Are of imagination all compact:
> One sees more devils than vast hell can hold,

> That is, the madman: the lover, all as frantic,
> Sees Helen's beauty in a brow of Egypt:
> The poet's eye, in fine frenzy rolling,
> Doth glance from heaven to earth, from earth to heaven;
> And as imagination bodies forth
> The forms of things unknown, the poet's pen
> Turns them to shapes and gives to airy nothing
> A local habitation and a name.
>
> *A Midsummer Night's Dream*

Here, Shakespeare places the poet alongside the madman and the lover, one who imagines things that are not there, the other captured by a single image, cautions him on how to use his mind. It should begin by roaming expansively, fearlessly, without obsessive attachment, must 'glance from heaven to earth and earth to heaven'.

There is much freedom here, to make sketches, to extend imaginative reach, to embody forms, to place what is unseen before the eyes; to permit the emergence of a creative act, the material instrument, the pen, the poet's pen that places on the blank page phrases, words, musical notes, punctuation marks, is allowed to build up something where before there was no something and give to 'airy nothing a local habitation and a name'.

Is there not also some subtle advice about the company we keep? About veering too much to one side where we are rubbing shoulders with the madman? Or the other side where obsessive love distorts what we see?

Our earliest experiences are wordless. They are not soundless. A foetus can hear. To the newborn, words convey no meaning. Passing from womb to wider world, this little person's senses are probably like the various parts of a solar system in the early stage of formation. Like the various planets, the senses have not yet differentiated themselves, not achieved a definable separateness. This liminal world will relinquish most of its luminosity; a face and breast transformed into a person; sounds will become heard and spoken words; alphabets or ideograms acquire a sonic or visual form. And so on. Here, I am not attempting to be extensive or comprehensive. Others may wander here but I lay a claim to this ground to be the (not exclusive) province of poetry. This is where poetry is well equipped to travel. It is into this region that the poet ventures, if and when and only when he is fit to journey into the origins of his own self; and if he knows that the journey he has embarked upon is not merely one of exploring another's life, but it is also one that is a creation of his own soul.

In the Beginning

Coral Bay Western Australia

With outstretched arms face down we float,
Above a coral garden filled with liquid life.
Curves and lines below are strangely still.
We hover above flowers in perpetual
Bloom, as if a master mason had
Chiselled them from rock their giant petals
Always open while small fish – some blue, some
Translucent – like bees above feed and tend
Their garden. Our visiting time is brief,
This window into our past sea life fleeting.
We glimpse far-distant seasons. This beauty
Is for eyes alone. No sound, no breeze blown
Scent. Not ever to be touched.

Yours Sincerely

On reading *Grave Goods* by Helen Taylor Robinson

Grave Goods is a book I never want to finish,
And never will. I read aloud pleased my voice
Did magnify your words that were not words,
Portals rather, messengers from the unseen,
The untouched, the unimagined. The soul's
Striations. Like glaciers we descend life's valley,
Dissolve and are as one in oceans' arms.

'In the beginning' is a powerful set of words that recall for me the book of Genesis and St John's gospel, which are followed in the first by 'God created the world', and in the second by 'was the Word and the Word was with God and the Word was God'. And I found in Latin the musicality of both sentences even more powerful.

Here, I attend to creativity with a small 'c' and word with a small 'w'. Inner creativity is, I believe, a necessity for a sound mind and productive life, which strangely can often be evidenced by doing nothing, by holding back, not reaching for the untouchable, not touching the unreachable and participating in the mystery of life by dissolving within it.

Using the title 'Yours Sincerely' indicated that I was signing off on a letter. I had received Helen's book of poems *Grave Goods*, read aloud and allowed them to flow over me. Somehow, they all blended into one and I wanted to say thanks and wrote and sent the poem as thanks.

Nothing more needs saying about the other poem as it is simply what I 'saw' while snorkelling in Coral Bay, WA.

Silence

Silence Streams

Like an aurora, silence streams across the sky,
And though I cannot see or touch it passing by,
And people say it's nothing, simply absent sound
My inward ear still hears and wonders why.

Silence can be golden, hold a precious hue.
Why not pink or purple, caramel or cobalt blue?
It is not one but many, and its spectrum loud and soft
Can fill a million galaxies and morning's drops of dew.

Gift your silence colour, play with rainbow light,
Gift your silence texture, weave it fine or tight,
Gift your silence freedom, let it wildly roam
And search for hidden spaces, where it will ignite

And touch the infinite. Let it the frame'ed portrait,
The unframed face, sun's rise and set, commemorate.
Release your silence to your senses; touch and
Hear its dormant seeds awake to green and propagate.

Silent Man

No. It is a man said the mother to her child
whose arm and hand and small finger pointed
from the river bank
but he was here yesterday
and the day before said the mother
but why is he standing in the middle of the water?

Why does he not move?
Hearing no reply a small hand squeezed tighter
a small head looked upwards to a mother's face
large eyes silent and still gazed upon the man
soft words floated out on the breeze.

The child reached up and plucked them from the air
he's waiting. The waters of his world have been changeable of late
what was a modest flow increased torrents raged and white
waters raced down pushed forward through the narrow valleys.

Mercifully for a time all was quiet but his promise of peace
was broken and wrath and vengeance rode upon the waves
for many hours he was almost submerged
many watched and feared he would lose his footing
you can see even now it is far from calm.

Mother he just stares upstream up the mountain
why don't you call out louder mother tell him we are here
tell him…
…there is no need my child he knows he is not alone
once upon a time someone somewhere held his hand.

The Painter

Lost in her own stare the silent land was all
Breeze-waves on grass, on corn,
Swooping peregrine, rising waterfowl,
All stilled in that contracted stare,
In watercolour framed, pronounced eternal.

Strangely, writing on silence is a special challenge. Some poems are written about the subject silence. Some are structured to convey silence. We have experience of many types of silence that can range from a sense of total openness, freedom and lightness to using all the adjectives that convey the opposite.

Vermeer's paintings can hold a stillness and silence that I find inspirational and I can endeavour to lift the people he painted from the canvas with words and give them a breath of life. That I try in 'The Painter'. 'Silence Streams', on the other hand, is a rambunctious dance with silences.

'Silent Man' has reflective, expectant, fearful, sinister, loving, hating, despairing, mute-screaming silences. Reading words from a page or screen is a silent act. But many poets write to be read out loud.

If you had wings and could fly (and let's add invisibility to your powers), you might have just landed on the riverbank and found you were eavesdropping on the conversation. At the end, what do you do with yourself? Fly away? Stay and hope for more? Or are you just staring at the silent man? Or are you the silent man?

'Silent Man' is written in such a way that you have to work out as you go along who is speaking, who is being spoken to, what is said out loud. Are words simply floating inside a mind? The eponymous man living up to his name? The poem, having already begun within an existing conversation, approaches its conclusion with rising urgency only to close with 'once upon a time'. And the suggestion of another story from long ago that may never be told. Or maybe you will tell it?

For Eyes Only

Fringe Dweller

Staffs of life are to her abhorrent.
With unwavering gaze and resolute lips
With hollow cheeks and shrunken limbs
To numb her gnawing need she strides
With flailing arms a moving crucifixion.

Imitating Art

Like needles piercing silk
Pointed blackwood trees
Pierced the glass lake.

(A painted ship upon
A painted ocean
Sailed into view.)

The leafless branches,
Brittle, silvered,
Seemed man-made

Structures. Thin bars
Of steel, protruding,
Sculptured, sparse.

   Perhaps the art and craft of the painter continues into these two poems. Written for the eyes, the subject matter is very different.' Imitating Art' might be described as a still-life poem. Nothing moves. Even the painted ship, despite having sailed into view, is caught inside a painting. The scene from which I wrote, Winneke, a lake-reservoir in Victoria, literally stopped me in my tracks as I walked past. I was transfixed. And am each time I reread or recite it. My guide/friend on the walk called it a dream place.

   The real fringe dweller, on the other hand, as week in week out, year after year, she pounded the pavements in the early mornings, conveyed a sense of persecuted power. If, for the briefest moment, you lifted your eyes and looked in her direction, you'd meet a sense of volcanic eruption. The elements to create the scene of the poem are garnered from peripheral vision and from the imagination. And from those who slowed the endless motion to sit and talk.

But even where there is minimal interaction, there is no escape from the pain, the loneliness that devours the spirit. An image of crucifixion is unbelievably painful. The image has been repeated through the centuries and evokes great sorrow; its contemplation possible if it touches our own suffering. But for how long could you look at a flailing arm, a moving nightmare, when the movement itself is an effort to dispel pain?

Miniatures

Real Presence

Your spirit at my side
absent footprints
in the snow.

Mirror Image

Don't look away
I wasn't staring.
I saw my youth in you.
    That's all.

Sea Creatures

Shoals of memories
Moments of our past
Swim the oceans of our lives
We who are wanderers
Mingle with the currents
Let those who stand
Safe upon the shore
Cast the nets

These poems are so brief the less said about them the better. They are meant to be little explosions in the mind. They can easily be retained in memory. Sometimes, short poems are so spare the reader can feel inclined to rush in to stop it falling over. Suffice it to say that making them can take a long time. Sometimes – I referred to this earlier – there may have been no intention to write a short poem, but when the long one seemed close to completion, there was realisation that already, a few lines inside the poem said it all. The superfluous are discarded and there you have it. Like getting off work early!

Finally, the risk of producing an aphorism should be watched, because, without care, it will descend into an 'I' on the page, to no one's advantage.

Play With Time

The Eternal Now

When
> I place a seashell upon your hand;
> stand at your side and stare at a yellow sunset;
> the moon paints our faces silver-white;
>
> I point to the pink hibiscus;
> say the tea has a hint of peppermint
> and you should try it;
>
> I want you to close your eyes
> listen to a Heaney poem
> a song by Joni Mitchell or Leonard Cohen;
>
> I take your hand and we walk in the bush
> inhale moist air overladen
> with sweet eucalyptus;

I see a moment of your birth my child,
I meet a moment of my death my child.

Time travel intrigues. *Star Wars*, warp speed, machines to travel in. Yet, get inside a poem and you may be taken across, let's say, the Butterfly Nebula, normally a journey of three light years, and you could make the journey in no time at all.

Poetry is a great explorer.

And meanwhile, back on planet Earth that holds us to it, each individual belongs to a relay team. We take the baton that is life when given, do the best we can and pass it on. Our piece of time can be counted in its years. Best in moments.

And so, we play with time, play with inhabiting a single solitary moment of our existence, one that will never, can never, be known by another, such is the nature of human self-consciousness. And then we move out, towards the furthest reach of another's emotional existence, searching for companionship, for the giving and receiving of gifts.

Word Painting

Maternal Light

Hand me a canvas and I will mark your outline
standing beside the bedroom window
I stared at the ceiling as the night began
to drain the light from the day
your sign to step into the shape you made
the night before and the night before that
and always when I turn and lean on my elbow
I see you smile as you stare into your past your time
in Leeds and Bradford during the war the small suitcase
packed under the bed ready to leave
at a moment's notice when the siren sounds
a siren has now swept you away forever
your outline remains but the space inside
is emptied of all light and of all grace
and never again will you fill the place we shared
the space that held the fabric of my dreams

Small Beginnings

It was the hardest thing I did in my life
cracked my heart in two you said
leave four small children at the gate
turn and step into the old black Ford.

I can travel with you now
I sit beside the brown suitcase in the back seat
torrents of tears flowing your gaunt face promising
one day you will return to us.

Two years of our lives you lost
an iron will steered you back
complete with an ocean of love
that kissed the shores of all our lives for all our days.

Soon I will be twice the age you were when you departed
Now I am the tallest of them all then the smallest
and part of me stands still at the gate one hand inside
my trousers pocket the other in a brother's hand

the old black Ford splutters into life
moves through the avenue of beech trees
disappears behind the high hedge
falls over the edge of the earth.

The making of some poems occurs like a painter at his easel with slow concentrated construction. The blank canvas recedes and the image emerges from the shadows. Words, like brushstrokes, emerge; the picture on completion, to the poet, a surprise.

Some poems are painted before the first word arrives. The image is imprinted on the mind. The task here to find the words. If black and white have for you a power of their own, we would describe the challenge being to get the light right. If not, the colour of the words needs to be mixed.

It is a valid question to ask what our earliest memory was. But the answer given always recalls a visual image, even though our body has much earlier memories, bodily 'vivid' and everlasting.

Look back into a writer's past and search for traces of previous forms of expression. The image is often to be found between his words. Seeing with the eyes helps seeing with the mind. And there is a thread here which, if followed, can lead us back to pre-Homeric, pre- writing poets who relied heavily on word pictures to assist their own memory and to show their poems and stories to the listener.

Fun

134340

In 2006 scientists said Pluto
was no longer a real planet
and had to relinquish its name.
The celestial body became
binary dwarf planet 134330

Not to fast learned men and women of the skies.
We've known this little chap for a long time.
He's been part of the Solar family since 1930.
Is this how you deal with unwanted relatives?

Is it because he is a bit slow? I know
Mercury circles the sun in 88 days
and sister Venus in 288 so I guess
Pluto's 247 years could get on your nerves.
But is speed everything?

How would you feel if you were demoted
and lost your name, retired and given
a number to remember yourself by?
Pick on someone your own size
Jupiter or one of the other gas giants!

Have you no heart?
It's cold out there on the edge
sunlight takes six hours to arrive
and on a good day it is minus 230 degrees.
Someone's got to stand up for the small guy!

Some people are very good at writing funny, laugh-out-loud poems, explicitly humorous poems. This can lead to the formation of categories and positing a dichotomy between funny and serious. This is a misleading venture, in my view. The final poem's subject matter may be rightfully defined serious, but the making of the poem involved such exhilaration, such alchemic blending of words, phrases, images, punctuation, trials with sound that would replicate a quartet, even an orchestra tuning up, and finally the sheer joy upon completion making nothing less than a tragedy, an error of judgement, were the label of seriousness to be stamped upon it..

Music

Perfect Pitch

It happened impromptu when the word impromptu
was beyond me. People would call to the house
there'd be talk, of the weather, of rheumatism
and lumbago, of who had died
and who had lately come into the world.

The violin case would open, the melodeon taken
from its box, tin whistles from the shelf.
Speech would cease. Eyes close
and voices turn to song.

That was fifty years ago. And today
I wait in silence and when I hear
the perfect pitch of stillness
I know the bow is on the string

fingers caress the keys, eyes
are closing and heaven's gate
is opening once again.

Muscae Volitantes

Staring into the middle distance
seeing nothing, lost in half a thought signalled
its entrance. It came from south by south-west
and moved slowly upwards towards the centre of things.
It never arrived at its destination and disappeared
without trace or trail from the radar of my eye.

Over the years I grew familiar with its presence
and absence. I drew attention to it when a new pair
of reading glasses was required.
She called it a floater – *muscae volitantes*
a Pluto moving mysteriously
alone, away in the far-out regions.

A lilac tree grew at the gable end of our home
beside the garage and when possessed of abundance
it filled the air with perfumed delight.
A walk within the gravitational force of its affections
dispelled the farmyard odours of cow-dung and diesel.
Peering upwards into its canopy of colour
lifted up my eyes from my six-year-old feet
that had stood on the engine oil that seeped
into the beaten broken earth of the garage floor.

Staring into the middle-distance desiring
nothing, my purple sun rises and descends
and cradles me within a waif-like stillness.
The compass of my heart trembles and silent
Whispers herald the approach
of a faint and distant fragrance.

> Mistakes have taught me to quell my appetite
> I will not turn to see or reach to touch
> or strain for sound. My body like a musical instrument
> has become attuned and when the lilac bow draws
> slowly up and down and plays on the strings
> of all my senses, I inhale incense from the heavens,
> and soar inside a single moment of eternity.

A return visit to a poem can reveal new riches. 'Perfect Pitch' has given much. Just as the music was unplanned and evolved from visit to visit, so too does poetry. No jagged entry, it arises out of and uplifts the heart that beats its ordinary beat. There is no show, no performance. Everyone stops, takes notice and becomes part of things and when the instruments have returned to their boxes and cases, airs and melodies remain to intermingle with the ordinary.

The title of my first book of poetry *The Lilac Bow* was taken from the poem 'Muscae Volitantes'. It is one of the first I wrote. I place it here under the heading of Music because of where the poem progresses to; to the scent of the lilac and the sound of the violin becoming one. I can't pass without commenting further and speak of the satisfaction upon rereading old poems that still speak to you. In it are themes that I have returned to again and again. And it doesn't bring a sense of traipsing over old ground. I could have written it yesterday. On a farm, every year you plough the same land. But no ploughing is ever the same. It is the first step towards planting seeds that renew. That old themes are returned to again and again is neither here nor there while words bring forth new life.

In the 1986 T.S. Eliot Memorial Lectures, Seamus Heaney said poetry has a special status among the literary arts, that 'the poet is credited with a power to open unexpected and unedited communications between our nature and the nature of the reality we inhabit'.

In *Crediting Poetry*, Heaney referred to the

> temple inside our hearing which the passage of the poem calls into being…It has as much to do with the energy released by linguistic

fission and fusion, with the buoyancy generated by cadence and tone and rhyme and stanza, as it has to do with the poem's concerns or the poet's truthfulness.

There are sound chambers in the mind and body. Before we could speak, we were spoken to. We listened in the womb before we saw. But take us all back, way back, back years we count in millions. What entered the temple of our hearing them? In our early- or pre-human manifestations, what did we hear and listen for? How do we account for the way nature and all its sounds can draw us in and make us one?

Douglas Penick has written,

Music emerges from our longing intoxicated with sound.
Poetry emerges from longing intoxicated with language…
In music sound is structured to convey the depths of silence; in poetry
Language is arranged to convey truths and intensities beyond words.

Points of View

We Don't Talk These Days

We don't talk these days the way we used to
and when we do it seems one-sided
I supply the words she the listening.

The other day there was something
I wanted to tell her. It had to do with plates
dinner plates blue patterned dinner plates with

a country scene in Japan or is it China
a scene of mountains trees and gardens
tea-gardens and a small human figure
stands beside a bridge or gate or lake
a figure so small you could
if you're not careful not see it at all.

Someone told me you shouldn't
look upon the scene from where you stand
it is better to observe from the little figure's
point of viewing there's a new angle
other things different things to see
there's more to find if you look that way
I was told. I wanted to tell her that.

I imagined when I spoke the widening eyes
lips parted in awe a child-like smile of wonder
at knowledge that was new. But, you know,
she did that all her life became the little figure
found a new angle saw things inside me
I didn't know were there.

It is a strange fact but true
the dead can be more present
do more seeing more listening
than the ones we call the living.

Our deepest thoughts do not lie at the surface but are to be found within the deepest layers of the mind. Not content with being broken up or presenting piecemeal, and refusing to answer urgent time demands, if we are to detect their approach, we need avert our stare and journey to the peripheries.

'We Don't Talk These Days' is witness to the valuable inheritance of being watched by another from a position oneself has not yet known to occupy.

The Act of Writing

The Gift of Writing

It began with a lead pencil and a crooked line
The teacher called diagonal. It ended with a book,
His name upon the dust cover.

He was taught to strive for
Sentences that rode the thermals,
Words that called like bugles
Or whispered softly in the ear.
Or in your steps stopped you still.

Someone said a pen can be
An artist's brush; you can paint,
Lay down shades of colour
Beyond the black and white.
So, as he did strive the child

Inside, tongue between teeth,
Hope riding high gripped
The pencil, pushed, prayed,
Implored the line –
Be straighter than the last.

The Gift of Words

Before runic script and alphabets
Parchment and paper before man learned
To write it was all talk.

They were so in love with
Listening and some it must be said,
With the sound of their own voice,
It never occurred to anyone
To write it all down.

But seriously, I hear someone say,
Don't we have enough to read,
If we had all that our shelves
Would overflow, our libraries
Would be chock-a-block?

To which I say Amen, except,
If I can have the last word,
Wouldn't it be nice to know
What the first one was?

I note the way this present sentence was first written. I note the old attachment to pen and paper and how something is released inside. I also recognise a certain peculiar reluctance to transfer to printed script. I can't really explain. A certain physical connection in holding the pen, moving it across the page? Perhaps some remnants of letter writing and receiving? I'll go with that. There is something here that the world and I are in danger of forgetting now that electronic forms of communication dominate distant personal communications.

A few issues here. Allowing for a choice of fonts, every electronic script is the same. But for most of my life I could tell who sent me a letter by their handwriting. I didn't need to turn over the envelope and read 'sender'. The presence of those who wrote to us revealed itself within the familiarity of the handwriting. And then there was the imagining: envelope being addressed, sealed, stamped and posted, sent on its way to the other side of the world to arrive in a postbox or droped through the letter flap.

Some letters were opened straightaway when picked up; the gratification from others delayed until by deliberate choice or intuitive action the best place and circumstance, in the house, garden or if early morning when you had gone back to bed with a cup of tea, the seal is broken and you plunge inside.

Being a personal document, the reading was rarely rushed. And often as not, the letter would have been written in a manner altogether impossible for an electronic device. At the end, where paper space had run out, the PS began, the afterthought written vertically up the margin of the page, across the top upside-down, and down the other side, while the smaller and smaller script, which required lifting the letter closer to the eyes, might convey sadness that this side of the conversation was drawing to its inevitable close, mingled with the anticipatory joy that you would 'write soon'.

We can't of course reverse time. Were we to, all books would become manuscripts. But instead of losing ourselves in the dismissal of the absurdity, perhaps, as is the case with many things, the honest acknowledgment of a loss may point us in a new direction, a new location where the regaining of a precious form of human contact might make its way to us from beyond the previously known boundaries of our imagination.

Listening

Old Ground

He had no more need of days and weeks and months,
The particular year was of no account, and when asked
To name the prime minister of Australia he declined.
Mind you, these days that changed so often, if found
Not to know he would be forgiven and excused.

He stepped back from all these minor matters and retreated;
Not so much a retreat as a return. He had no need
For walls and doors; no love of the high-rise.
His was open ground (where anyone could come and go)
Ground that had since time immemorial been walked

Upon and watched over, tended and sown by poets.
Here once the spoken word had reigned supreme,
The music and the sight of sound repeated from
Generation to generation. Here words were first
Chiselled into rock. Here parchment and berry ink

Came into vogue. Manuscripts and books arrived,
And the printing presses, and then the internet.
He didn't care. They were all the same to him,
All means to an end. Surrounded by riches
Every morning he just sat and waited while

Seeds scattered by the world's poems germinated,
Sprouted, made flowers and leaves and branches
And full-grown trees. And when the sun danced
Upon his face or the moon silvered his already
Silver hair, or the wind blew louder and longer

Than had been foretold, or darkness removed all
Curves and lines and demarcations, it mattered
Not at all. And if he spoke little it was not he had
Nothing to say. He was past the waste of time.
He just waited. There was so much listening to do.

Imagine you have a large sheet of paper. On it, draw a large circle. At the centre of the circle, make a small circle. In the space between the two, write in all the human capacities, traits and qualities you hold dear and consider important in life. Now move the one you consider most important into the small circle.

The capacity I locate in the centre is the capacity to listen. How many people do you know who really listen to you? How often do you really listen to someone else? It is a deeply demanding thing to do. Listening to conduct business or acquire factual information is simple; the personal is minor or non-existent. But where the personal is major, when sympathy and empathy are required, even with the best will in the world, we can fall short.

Not I

I will never look into your eyes

After London, 7 July 2005

On the last night sleep is far from me
Distant sounds empty of all colour
Gather to announce my end.
I will never look into your eyes.

I dress for my last day
I cover my body with the garment of death
I pass the mirror in my room.
I will not look into my eyes.

I walk beside you into the waiting train
I see you smile as you touch a hand
You will never touch again.
I cannot look into your eyes.

A father dries the tears of a crying child
A baby drinking from his mother's breast
Turns to me.
I will not look into his eyes.

A girl in blue stands smiling
In her hand the hallowed book
I blow them all to blood and dust.
I will never look into her eyes.

They say I will be counted holy
They promise a seat among the blessed
But I have slain both young and old
Stolen the life of a new-born child.
How will I look into His eyes?

Lending your 'I' to a terrorist who blows to pieces or burns to death babies, children, mothers, fathers, ordinary people, people of his own faith, lovers, all in the name of a loving God, is not an easy task.

I helped myself through this piece of writing by using a chorus line to end each stanza. It was like a steel bar you hang on to in a gale. It was a steadying device as I shadowed him on his murderous path, sat beside him, sat beside all those who were full of their lives that were soon to be extinguished. The slaughter, the carnage, the terror, the suffering is indescribable. And there are those who survived who to this day live with the disabilities and the pain inflicted upon them. And writing something in this manner, the poet is concerned for the readers, for leaving them to imagine scenes he left undescribed.

Space-time

What is it about Space-time? Do you know? Or like me, have you gently let it slide to the side of your mind, as being beyond you, hoping that maybe one day, you will achieve enlightenment? Or a newer, larger intelligence? The problem is not out there. That some are capable of understanding that which, to me, is at present a mystery would suggest it's to do with the way I look at things.

One way of progressing is to place the problem to one side and find an analogous situation to explore or an allegory to step inside. It can be a tricky move. Some, while inside the analogy or allegory, feel they have reached some understanding. But it is a pseudo-understanding. A self-deception. They have failed to return to the place where the presenting problem was parked and failed to make a renewed effort to understand it. Group discussions on challenging emotional issues often perpetuate and sanction this deception.

Don't let that prevent you from exploration like this. I think my problem in comprehending space-time is like the one that existed in the human mind before it could conceive of the numeral 0. Before 0 could be thought of, things could only be as 1 or more. Something had to be in a space to have existence. A nothing was beyond comprehension. If an opening presented itself a thing, 1 or more was automatically placed within it. The thing placed was a thing that existed. Efforts to see beyond were believed to be impossible. A way to describe this is to think of life before airflight. Walking on the earth, you can only see up to the horizon. Even if you move about, even if you know the earth is round, you can never actually see over the horizon. Your eyes and brain are confined to what's visible.

Therefore, is it that when we say I can't conceive of space-time, we have accepted the limits of our capacity, in the same way the earth-bound man accepts he can't see beyond the curve?

Now what about space-time in here, inside the mind?

Listen to Proust.

When a man is asleep, he has in a circle around him the chain of the hours, the sequence of the years, the order of the heavenly bodies. Instinctively he consults them when he awakes and in an instant, reads off his own position on the earth's surface and the time that has elapsed since his slumbers…

Proust goes on to describe waking not knowing where he was or, worse, who he was, feeling destitute. Relief came when he realised where he was, and that connection to a place was 'like a rope let down from heaven to draw me up out of the abyss on non-being, from which I could never have escaped by myself' [and I was helped to] 'gradually piece together the original components of my ego'.

Now listen to Karl Haas.

We tend to categorise all works of art according to their time of origin. Somehow, our power of perception seems to function better if we are able to think in terms of chronological order. It is as if viewing an art object, reading a work of literature, or listening to a musical composition triggers a subconscious reaction, revealing all the sensory experiences that we associate with any given stretch of history. If any new creative encounters elude our imaginary card-file of classification, we have difficulty assimilating them.

Questions. Do we struggle with space-time out there because we struggle with space-time in here? I have no answers but I have learned something. That the mind has its limitations, that to stay in the game we must stay connected to some sense of 'being' because we are not in the game lost in 'non-being'. My rope is my acceptance of mystery? I think this is inadequate. And a premature departure. I sense I can go further, so I'll try. Drawing on Proust's 'rope let down from heaven', I ask, is creativity the rope? Is non-being a prerequisite for a creative act? Can nothing come from nothing? Or something? Is Haas's new musical creator required to empty his mind of the sequence of the years of music, detaching himself from the sensory experiences he has previously been exposed to? Disassemble classification? And listen?

If the abyss of non-being is entered into with hope and faith that listening is opening space for creativity, we are not alone. The mystics and the great poets are not far away. And we are in the company of great writers like William Hazlitt, who advised that a man should 'open his senses, his understanding, and his heart to the resplendent fabric of the universe'.

In all other instances, I offered the poems first. Not so here.

Departed Virtue

In the midst of the bustling crowd
Jesus said who touched me

and the woman with the issue of blood
confessed she stole his virtue.

How do we know who takes
and who is moved by a delicate
need for grace?

Seeing Things

Sometimes it seems the soul's so vast,
Streaming on its path from day of birth,
Fine-woven from invisible threads to last,
From babe's first cry until the hour of death.
Sometimes to me, it seems, once born
Imagination, gazelle-like moves in bounds,
Journeys, like prayer, without fear of scorn,
Through silent worlds in search of distant sounds.
Sometimes, ourselves we strive to teach.
Fate's more powerful and can trump design,
What's most glorious is always out of reach,
Like life itself: a mystery, gifted and benign.
On a well-greased weighbridge, we balance all our being,
One glance made glorious; all else by us unseen.

Are We There Yet

He owned his own church. It was small –
like St Kevin's at Glendalough in County Wicklow
Ireland or the Church of San Carlos Borroméo
at Carmel in Monterey County California –

and it was very beautiful. It wasn't real, of course.
No. It was complete in his mind,
so he could take it with him
all the time, wherever he went.

He would slip away when he was with me,
I never noticed because
when I talked and he listened
he gave his full attention.

And it was only later after he'd gone
for good only then did I know his church
was a place he had often taken me to that his church
was a place we'd been together in silent prayer.

The Gift of Being

To be,
Or never to have been,
Not how, or Who created
The simple fact of Being,
That the animate and inanimate
Are.

If you think I have been playing with your mind, you are correct. Not idly, but for a purpose. If I had offered a poem or poems with a religious flavour or association and you read 'Departed Virtue' and you had immediately identified the passage in Scripture that it referred to, even before you got to the end, your mind could be crowded with 101 associations. My reason for playing with your mind was to show how hard it can be to see and hear anew.

If you were born into that tradition, words like 'Jesus', 'church', 'prayer', can act like magnets that pull in a certain direction. Can the reader of 'Are We There Yet' allow the church to be 'complete in his mind'? Can the reader of 'Departed Virtue' contemplate questions such as these: is the trust you place in a person whom you believe can help you a vital part of healing? How does the act of secretly taking from another differ from openly asking and differ from being driven by need? If the giver of grace works in mysterious ways, how does the one that is given to receive the gift?

The psychoanalyst Wilfred Bion's work led him to conclude that the mind of mankind grows not by increasing factual knowledge but through encounters with ultimate reality, everlasting loneliness, the pain made bearable by the beauty of the universe. And we can turn to Kahlil Gibran.

> When you love, you should not say 'God is in my heart,' but rather, 'I am in the heart of God'. And think not you can direct the course of love, for love, if it finds you worthy, directs your course.

4
Poetry in a Time of Pandemic

Now to the smaller story within the larger story. John Keats said poems should come like leaves falling from trees. I was, as I said, surprised when, looking back from 2021, that from the beginning of the pandemic, I had written more poems than in any similar period of my life. Somehow in the midst of all the uncertainty and disruptions to life, I had found space to see some falling leaves.

Poems, as I have described, begin with a phrase, an image, a melody in words; they arrive, as Keats said, unannounced. Following the initial flash of inspiration, the making of the piece of art which is the finished poem takes time and hard work, as I have also described. And what I call 'soft' work, softly following the initial flash, probing the origins of the poem, releasing an energy that has been unconscious, dormant, awaiting release and an opportunity to achieve shape, form and expression. Poems that signpost the inner world offer ways to understand ourselves.

In a time when enormous efforts were extended dealing with external threats, we needed to also attend to our internal world. What did the pandemic touch within? To where were we taken? What nights from our past did we revisit? What figures returned in our dreams? Did dreams collapse into nightmare?

Time itself underwent many distortions and convulsions as we were deprived of the places, people and activities that normally characterise and shape everyday life. Poems like 'Al-jabr' and 'Scattered Images Seeking Form' will attend to disorientation, to regaining our mind and capacity to think. The presence of death around us could not be avoided and you will read how it was faced in 'This Situation' and 'Endings'. However, we were also in the presence of life and poems about that life, and what sustains and nurtures it had to be written. The same leaves fell, the same rivers ran, day followed night. When the past called out, it needed to be imaginatively revisited, the creative space of dreaming re-established, our inner compass reset.

If the spirit of poetry waned in some quarters under the strain of the pandemic, a shaft of light illuminated the darkness when on 8 October 2020 the Nobel Prize for Literature was awarded to the American poet Louise Glück, for her 'unmistakable poetic voice that with austere beauty makes individual existence universal'. I will say more about her later.

In the *Odyssey*, Odysseus instructed his crew to strap him to the mast so he could hear, but not succumb to the terrifying beauty of the Sirens' song. To strap oneself to the mast was a frequent necessity in the pandemic. The same action was necessary to get these poems onto the page. To see the initial flash, the image, hear the music in words, you have to attend. Then, with pen in hand, indentured to the task, poems were made.

Virtually all the poems began in 2020 and 2021. A few had earlier origins, but were reimagined and rewritten. In a year when the hold on life itself was fragile, a hold many lost, the truth about the ordinariness and the quintessence of that life had to be captured. The next group of poems are my experiments to grasp clearly and hold lightly true encounters of living through a pandemic.

Confusion

Al-jabr

In the ninth century an Arabian mathematician
Rose high in the sky.
As he soared an original idea came to him
And he made formulas for abstractions.
He called it al-jabr.
His name was Al-Khwarizmi.

Dear Mr Al-K,
The tilt of earth's axis has increased,
Or decreased. We cannot tell.
The planet's gravitational pull
May have weakened because
We have slipped over the horizon,
Beyond the circumference
Of the known.
It's scary out here.
It's very quiet.
The only sounds heart beats.
We need your help.
We need someone to rise and soar.
We need new formulas for our abstractions.
And a nice new name!
Thank you.

Job's Book

'God give me the patience of Job',
Was how I first heard the name.
And later when I read his book saw
Job was a man much wronged.
You could forget any sense of
Natural justice when his name came up.
There are a few books in the Biblical Canon
Deemed troublesome. Ecclesiastes – too agnostic.
Esther – forget to mention God.
The Song of Songs – too sexy.
And Job – the arbitrary cruelty
Of God too offensive.

Having taken everything bar life
From this blameless man,
His wife, his children, his livelihood, his health,
God, at the end restores everything to Job.

Excuse me! That was one great *deus ex machina*!
Now as Covid-19 swirls around us all
And justice frays at the edges,
You may find some consolation
Reading Job's book, The Book of Job.
Or you may not. Reality can be cruel.
The book of him is the book of us.
And who's to say you won't say,
'God give me the patience of Job.'

Scattered Images Seeking Form

Burnt and twisted trees like liquorice
Sticks. Ink-blot clouds.
Fractures in a crimson sunset.
Streams of motionless lava burn the sky.
Red-river gums reach to infinity
upside down inside wetlands pond.
Rusted windowless 1950s car
in rusted field of windswept grass.
Golden ash and claret ash
overflow the camera lens.
Each and all in time and place complete.
Mine the desire; the need for form.

Sometimes, without noticing it, we speak not with one but many voices. I wrote 'Al Jabr' with that conscious sense of bewilderment that came in the first months of the pandemic. But on rereading the finished poem, I detected another, younger voice politely pleading for help. To learn algebra, one needed to discover and to open a new chamber in the mind. Those mathematical symbols represented something else. If you haven't made your way into the chamber that has knowledge of symbolisation, you will remain confused. To enter it is an Archimedean moment.

I, we, the peoples of the world needed a new chamber in our individual and collective minds to comprehend what was unfolding.

Job's God was unpredictable and non-discriminatory. God played a deathly game with Job and killed his children and ruined his livelihood. It is an age-old story of arbitrary forces causing untold suffering. The pandemic was 'the plague', 'the pestilence' by a different name. At the middle of 'Scattered Images Seeking Form', everything is upside-down. The world's shape and form has slipped. Disparate images crowd the mind; a poem an attempt to catch hold of scattered emotions and ideas.

Presence of Death

Endings

When told that time was short
He'd best prepare for death,
He said, 'Ah well, more of the same'.

Life was not for him a flood of light
From the beginning. A candle flickered
Whose flame he learned to tend,

Or the lighthouse beam was waited for.
Shadows always stood around,
Darkness seemed to own more ground.

'Too much optimism,' he also said,
'Weighs you down. Hope uplifts.
You float among the fragile,

The transient, the lighter essence
On the scales of honest love
Matters most. When every breath

Is weighed as if the first,
As if the last, we can all say,
Ah well, more of the same?'

This Situation

This situation I find myself in was not meant to be.
The old we are told are first in line to go, and you can
See old age has not yet wrinkled me. But now
I have been told I am shifted up the queue.

This has struck me as unjust, and the axes
Of my universe do not now align. But this is where
I find myself. Until I am required what am I to do?
Curse the fates, the gods, the elements?

Submit to grief? By sorrows be caressed?
Place me among trees and flowers,
Because it's where the days and hours
I've left are better spent. There I'll rest.

When my words cease, recall our first hello,
Our uncountable hours of talk, that we loved
And worked with zest. And when stock was low
How well we husbanded the interest.

Most of all keep mirth alive; we laughed more
Than we cried. And when my spirit re-presents,
Lift your eyes, forget your toils, and forbid not
Falling tears when they mingle with your smiles.

One among the many distresses that the pandemic inflicted was people having to die alone, being unable to say goodbyes; not only was death hastened, final words could not be exchanged. For some, death is an ending lived for, meaning the way they live their life is the way they die; it's a fact they account for. 'Endings' depicts such a situation. 'He' has long ago experienced the fragility of life, and frequently weighed his options, life's lightness, its transience leading not to fear but a finer appreciation of its essence. I have gone back to this poem substituting 'I' for 'He'. Try it!

In 'This Situation', death is untimely and unprepared for. Nevertheless, the subject, having addressed the inevitable, speaks those parts of the exchange and manages to make the absent present and bring them to life.

Many in the pandemic were not so lucky. Nobody to place them 'among trees and flowers'. No one to whom they could speak the last two stanzas.

Making Space

Elbow Room

A bit of elbow room, the space to turn.
Time to open wide or squint
Or see beyond what's seen.

Indifferent – to the words that twist and
Turn and race behind white-water rapids.
Patient – to await the dancing songs

Which skip on streams to kiss
The scattered stones and sands.
Songs, that were sung by birds ten,

Twenty, thirty million years away
Drift – like seeds with wings that float
Far off from trees – through time.

I've always needed elbow room,
To open space, to step outside,
To feel the breeze refresh my face.

Finding the Perpendicular

All this hurly-burly
The sight, the sound, the sense of things,
The rambling clouds, piercing rays, the
Hurricanes of thought.

What will happen if they never
Are recorded, nowhere reach a shape,
And like crashing waves their form
To formlessness unwitnessed?

And will anything remain in the morning?
It's no matter. They are neither mine
Nor yours to possess. But turning
To look out the window at 2 a.m.,
Beyond the trees, seeds of light
In the distance sown, in the dawn
I trust will germinate and bloom.
Is this the gift of life?

A threat to life can make us look inwards if lockdown restricts our minds as well as our bodies. 'Elbow Room' breaks free in all directions and takes off as far as thirty million years away. This is a celebration after confinement, of finding an open space 'to step outside / To feel the breeze refresh my face'. 'Finding the Perpendicular' is finding the compass of mind when its arrow swings wildly, and welcoming the quiet, the stillness of the night. The sun is at the other side of the globe, and the thoughts we wrestle with unformed. In time, they 'will germinate and bloom', if we have trust in the gift of life.

Both poems call back to 'Al jabr' and 'Scattered Images Seeking Form'. Now, formlessness is not feared. The need for others to perform a miracle subsides when we have carried out the necessary repairs on our own mind.

Defiance

Defiance

Once, in the Gulag in the freezing food line
A woman stood beside Anna Akhmatova,
Is your poetry strong enough for this?
Once, an IRA man toting a gun eyeballed Seamus Heaney,

When for fuck sake will you write something for us?
Poems' powers outlast the tyrants'; they who do not
Pause to grieve, their empty eyes and blood-
Stained lives conceal the bloodless life within.

Shoot or starve the poet, another rises tools of trade
In hand, defying fear and death. Defying Gulag and
Gun. Word by lithesome word erected.
Defying gravity. Defying silence.

Of Birds and Poets

A bird who dies in flight falls vertical through cloud,
Small heart that beat a trillion beats grows tired,
Slender strength dissolves, wings falter, cease to glide
Plummets to the ground. A ragdoll cast aside.
But a strange thing happened. (My eyes I fear deceived),
The arms of earth extend, a great wanderer received.
Earth – many trillion tonnes to its bosom holds the tern
Who weighs a hundred grams. As a breeze will sway a fern,
Or rustle leaves on tree tops, as mist bejewels snowdrops,
As sparrow's fall, to this life's end, the call to us – attend.

A poet who dies respected, his words like silver rays
Is cherished and remembered and lights up all our days.
Liu Xiaobo died imprisoned and was cast into the sea,
They hoped he'd be forgotten, unloved, by you and me.
But a strange thing happened. The sea rejected lies
And from his ashes strewn a flock of birds now flies.
There's one in every tree and all corners of the land
Are by a canopy of silver singing spanned.
Liu Xiaobo's life is lost, him we all must mourn,
But as we read his poems his spirit is reborn.

He said the darkness one day will cease,
We'll wake to freedom's songs of peace.

Free Speech

Speech is free to the child
Who needs to wail and moan,
And to the young who have not
Learned the weight of words,
For whom an unseen sun and
Glowing moon are one.

Speech is free to a frail old mind,
When life's achievements sink and fade,
When words, thoughts, imaginings,
Waiting, listening, learning, leisurely
Half-knowing, ecstasy on seeing,
Have lost their place in its firmament.

Others, from president to pauper pay
The price: indentured to the words they use,
Paraded before the gods of poetry,
Those ancient pre-mind forms,
Who carved the shapes of words,
To carve the shapes of minds.

The Assembly Line

Strolling on pebbled shores gathering
Words like shells and stones
Until your pocket fills and overflows.
Punctuations, rhythms, rhymes
And half-rhymes, whole phrases spill.

A stanza flowers, withers and dies.
A villanelle forms, its parts won't bind.
Like sprites on foam free verses dance,
Like sirens a sonnet sings, to sea
Spray's dashed a haiku's wings.

Distraught you stumble, the pocket
And you are empty. Or so it seems.
In the soggy fabric, caught in a fold
Moonlight makes a gemstone shine.
That image, that scent of morning

That got you going, glistens. In the
Gloaming, in dreaming it lays down roots.
Like a pendulum to the flow and ebb
Of tides, your words can sing and chime.
Beware deracination. Beware thieves of rhyme.

In *Pandemics and Society: From the Black Death to the Present*, emeritus professor of history and the history on medicine Frank M. Snowden has explored pandemics, plagues and pestilences through history. In the *Dublin Review of Books*, July 2021, a reviewer, Eoin O'Brien, wrote the following.

> The devastation caused by past pandemics can be attributed more to the incompetence of government and the misuse of available preventative treatment measures than to the virulence of infecting organism. Historical examination of pandemics…illustrates repeatedly that the behaviour of the most intelligent species on the earth, when faced with annihilation is often downright stupid.

I would add that the behaviour of the most intelligent species on the earth in pandemics can be downright horrifying. There are many instances in the book where the disturbance caused by a pandemic was used to exert power over vulnerable individuals and communities. We might all be familiar with the burning of women deemed to be witches and other cases of the outsider, or the one on the margins of society blamed and abused. It was used as an opportunity to settle old scores or commit atrocious crimes. Plague broke out in Milan in 1630. Milan was at war with Spain. Four Spaniards, in the wrong place at the wrong time, were apprehended and blamed for spreading the plague. They were tortured and their hands cut off before being burned at the stake.

One of the worst cases documented in the book was the treatment of Jews during an outbreak of the plague in Strasbourg in Alsace. The municipal authorities blamed the two thousand Jews living in the city for spreading the pestilence by poisoning the wells Christians drew their water from. On Valentine's Day 1349, they were rounded up and given the choice between conversion and death. Half became Christian. The remaining thousand were taken to the Jewish cemetery and burned alive.

If a pandemic sends the world upside down, our minds are sent upside down. Once the latter, our mind, has been righted, we recover our capacity to think, have set things in place to maintain our balance. We must attend to our world.

In our times of great anxiety and uncertainty, authoritarian individuals or regimes are using the opportunity to gain or extend power and autocratic rule. A poem can't provide any ready-made solutions, but it can illustrate the obstacles that impede and prevent thought and expression. The tyrant's fear of free speech is greater than his fear of weapons. He can amass more lethal weapons but he can't get his hands on the poem. The precious freedom, the liberty that a poem and a poet bear witness to, leaves the tyrant and his regime helpless, except to ban, imprison or kill the poet. But nothing can kill a poem. As in 'Defiance', no matter how hard life is, the poet speaks.

Why place 'The Assembly Line' here? Simply because all poems must be given the same attention, whether it deals with a daisy or a dictator. Words matter. Take care.

There is a wide sweep here, carrying the word 'free' aloft describing its different manifestations and iterations. And a reminder when, as far as we know, poems as made-up things first came into being (as in the times of the early Greek poets) when man's world, man's mind was populated with many gods. Through and with the gods, great stories were told of engagement with a domain 'beyond'. We can stumble with pre-mind forms while we carve 'the shapes of words to carve the shapes of minds'.

'On Birds and Poets', an elegy in a way to a brave poet, Liu Xiaobo. Like the smallest of birds, a poem is one of the smallest forms of writing. Amazing is it not the length to which nations with staggering military and economic powers will go in an effort to extinguish the light of freedom. But such power is no match for the flight of birds and poems.

A poem is the most useless and the most useful thing. It is worth nothing; it is worth everything. Learn to think about a poem. You will be able to think about anything. Poetry can describe what is seen to be. Poetry may suggest what is seen to be possible. In his Nobel lecture, given on 8 December 1979, the Greek poet Ulysseus Elytis said the following.

> It is not enough to put our dreams into verse. It is too little. It is not enough to politicise our speech. It is too much. The material world is really only an accumulation of materials. It is for us to show ourselves to be good or bad architects, to build Paradise or Hell. This is what poetry never ceases affirming to us – and particularly in these dürftiger times – just this: that in spite of everything our destiny lies in our hands.

Relearning to Think

Tracing Shadows

Shadows stretch further than we can go.
The woods, a magic place awaits. At his side
Another walks and together their shadows flow.

Have I been here before? He thinks, No,
But the sense of place swims deep inside
And shadows are seen stretching further than a child can go.

Seeing into long ago, seeing nature's morning show
Birds awakening, mist arising, safe and bleary-eyed
Beside another he stands. Their hands and shadows flow.

'I have…' she says, then seeks to keep the after-glow
Of recall bright, lest promised shapes elide
And dark consumes shadows where she will go.

'It was…' her eyelids close and she hears an arpeggio
Played on sunlit casuarina strings. With heart beguiled
She sings low, and finds herself where shadows flow.

Tonight, sleeping, dreaming you may see and know
A wood inside, a place that's fresh, free and rarefied.
Many shadows can search space where one won't go
Because side by side, together, our shadows glow.

A Compass Line of Light

A rudder holds a compass line of light.
A silver vessel silent on a silver sea.
An absent breeze the patient sails invite.

On distant shores two staring eyes alight,
Unknown, unnamed. It may be you. Or me
If the rudder holds our compass line of light.

Traversing far off lands can consume a life,
Always on the go, intrepid travellers we
Fear the absent breeze. Our impatient sails invite

Any forward thrust. Stillness is a plight.
Scanning flickering stars, we but faintly see
Our inner rudder's compass line of light.

A silver sea inside holds no fear of night.
Storms subside. The heart expectant, free,
No absent breeze desires. The patient sails invite

Time to heal, time to write, art to delight.
In poetry's vessel all faults pardoned be;
In tempest, its rudder our compass line of light,
Its breath the breeze our inner sails invite.

Dream's End

Sleeping to the beat of the night-owl's wing,
Walking through a dream in a dim-lit place,
Waiting for the dawn when lights will sing.

If ascending darkness leaves its sting
The heart's awash, the mind arace,
We won't hear the beat of the night-owl's wing.

Seeds' cradles be their graves. No spring
Swaps winter's depths for grace.
No new day dawns with lights that sing.

But dreams as maps of minds bring
To our inner eyes shapes that hearts erase,
To our ears soft beats of the night-owl's wing.

Dream music strums on silent string,
Dream art paints translucent face,
New days may dawn. Lights may sing.

Frightened, faithful, brimming
Eyes find paths through unbound space,
Trusting the beat of the night-owl's wing.
Inhaling dawns with lights that sing.

When first written, 'Tracing Shadows' had three clearly defined people. In stanza 2 and 3, a man and a woman walked into a wood. Their past sprung to life. The man remembered being there as a child with his father. Then in stanza 4 and 5, the woman spoke and remembered being there but the memory faded. She recaptured it when she closed her eyes and sang.

In mid-2021, I rewrote the poem in its present form. I had listened to a radio programme called *Alone with J.S. Bach*. In the US when the musical producer David Schulman was in lockdown with much time on his hands, he decided to research the Six Sonatas and Partitas for solo violin by J.S. Bach. He interviewed violinists around the world who loved and played Bach.

David Schulman had a facsimile of Bach's original score. I can't read – although I have seen – music sheets, but never anything like the first page, the opening adagio, from Bach's manuscript. Schulman called the manuscript 'a spell book' and described it as calligraphy. The violinist Rachel Podger found delight in what she described as notes written like squiggles. In this work, instead of including a viola, cello and bass, we hear a single 'voice', then two, then three simultaneously 'speaking', all on a single violin.

Speculations abound as to what Bach was trying to do. He composed it in 1720 after the sudden death of his wife Maria Barbara leaving him with four children under the age of thirteen. Perhaps he was recreating on one violin the talk between him and Maria Barbara and family chatter at mealtimes.

Composers of music leave words behind and delve into the human heart and mind, giving wordless expression to emotion and thought. The poet can compose a poem going the other way. My poem already had the line, 'she hears an arpeggio / Played on sunlit casuarina strings'. In the rewriting, I blurred the distinctions between different people and tried to emulate Bach, leaving the reader (as opposed to listener) to pay close attention and work out who and how many were speaking at any one time, and whether the conversation was aloud between two people, between a person and their child self, or silently to the self within the privacy of the mind. Maybe I'll never be able to read or recall this poem without Bach accompanying me in the background.

Unless we can hear the breeze, there is not a sound in 'A Compass Line'. We are in a 'silver vessel silent on a silver sea'. Neither is there a shadow. As the poem progresses, the silver is inside. Inner freedom comes with waiting. The belief that inspiration is a gift no one can command echoes through this book. And when received, there is 'Time to heal, time to write, art to delight'. That line, indeed all of the last stanza, echoes William Shakespeare's final work, *The Tempest*. In fact, it takes us to the final scene of the play. Prospero, having renounced all his false magic used to control and punish others, as he is about to leave the island of isolation, speaks his soliloquy. More on *The Tempest* later.

The coronavirus virus pandemic has literally given many people nightmares. Nightmares are failed dreams. We awake in fear and terror, as opposed to puzzlement. If fear persists and then sleep itself is feared, we need help. Whatever help we find has to return us to sleep and dreams. 'Dream's End' charts such a recovery.

Re-finding Old Discoveries

In Praise of Homework

For some the 60s were for living dangerously,
Drugs, sex, rock and roll. But in Ireland,
My Ireland, times were hard.
Farm workers abandoned the land for England's factories,
Crops rotted in the fields. And in '64
A television set was installed in my homework room.

I need silence to hear myself think,
Stillness without to see sights within.
So. Each evening when the light was slant
Something in me leaned towards that room.
I imagined sitting in my old place at the table
Beside my brother. I reach out to touch
That old wooden box turned on its side,
Which housed my little library
Books on Irish, English, history, geography,
Latin, maths, science. And patiently awaiting
My return, my tools of trade: pens, pencils,
Rubber, ruler, sharpener and geometry set.
Instruments to measure my world,
Give it line and shape and form.

Homework time is half about what's learned.
Half about a space where it's safe to tend
To seeds and shoots; watch blooms unfold,
Hear stirrings in your growing mind
That no one else can hear.
Escape the grey. Evade the black and white.

My Short Explanation of Almost Everything

Two friends who missed the science class
Asked what happened. Back then,
Had I the wit that I have now just
Stumbled on, I would have said,
We weighed Archimedes in water!

Our classroom was inside the science lab.
I stood beside the scales and set about
Repeating and explaining the
Experiment, weighing an object
In air and then in water.

I began with knowing – that knowing
You know but can't explain.
The same knowing that starts a poem.
Blind faith that sees where the spark
Strikes, the poem ignites.

In caves, on clifftops, under pebbles
And rocks, beneath searing sun and
Silent moon, inside clouds and storms,
Amid joys and sorrows words await.
They bide their time, drift, cascade, ride rapids,

Dance upon the surface of the mountains' streams,
Destined for the ocean. My words flowed bravely on
And when I arrived at the end of the experiment,
I can safely say I had done a wonderful job
Of explaining almost everything.

The circumstances and times of all our individual beginnings are like that place of the map we started out from. 'Going home', revisiting in memory and imagination the places and the people that we and others around us were, can, like a deep well, provide refreshments for all our life. Nostalgia and sentimentality often offer little. But when revisiting becomes a 'Remembrance of the Things Past', as outlined by Proust, the old is infused with new life and each time a return occurs accompanied by art, in this instance a poem, you can see and say things, which back then you never had words for. 'In Search of Lost Time', the alternative title of Proust's masterpiece, prompts me to think that a poet goes back, not so much in search of lost words as in search of old, lost images for which words until now have not been found. There is great satisfaction sitting where you used to sit and taking what was then out beyond the horizon of your mind – the content of the last stanza – and hauling it in, giving it new shape and form. Homework within 'In Praise of Homework' has become work that is conducive to remembering and repairing.

'A Short Explanation of Almost Everything' is about another moment that was not actually over the horizon but sat on its edge. The poem is about one of those small events you never forget. Actually, this was for me an important moment in learning about learning. When I had been asked what had happened in the previous lesson, I knew that I knew. Had a draconian teacher listened in to our conversation and demanded I explain, everything would have been ruined. I took a step closer that day towards knowing that there can be knowledge in the mind that is real and true, but the logical steps by which that knowledge can be shown to others – and even laid out systematically and sequentially for oneself – was yet to be found. In the instance in question, as I was demonstrating the experiment to my two classmates, I was simultaneously demonstrating and explaining it to myself.

A Return

Give Water Welcome

Lightning whitened sky
Thunder darkened sound
Rain-drenched face
And outstretched arms
Give water welcome.
Lines of people
Criss-cross the planet
Plunge back in time
To the first time
Lightning whitened sky
Thunder darkened sound
A rain-drenched face
And outstretched arms
Gave water welcome.

The Patience of Water

Not the rapid roar nor the
Unmeasurable power of a Niagara
Falls. I mean the slow meandering
Music, always in the low register
You hear or hope to hear
Stock still upon the stepping stones,
Or at the edge bent low
Drinking from a hand overflowing
With newborn silence.

Your lips have kissed, your fingers
Touched the history of life's universe
Beginning billions of years back
As other elements. Its music
Made the oceans deep, shaped the land
Reached to the skies, transformed itself to mist,
Steam, vapour, fog, rain, snow and ice.

Inside what plants and living creatures
Does it travel and remain? No breath,
No eye, can bear its absence.
Without it where would beauty be?
Raindrops, sea mist, snowflakes
Dew on grass and flower and leaf,
It sits invisible in air, eons inside a glacier,
Yet never does it say, look at me.
Such is the patience of water.

Four a.m.

At four a.m.
the street lights'
light like a little sun

passes through the window.
Shadow on the wall
a black and white photograph

of hedge and tree,
a once-off, one-person
view. Because tomorrow

at four a.m. the hedge
and tree like you will have had
a change, if ever so slight.

Evening

Evening light white
With a tint of yellow.
It won't be long now.

'Give Water Welcome' and 'The Patience of Water' are celebrations of how far-reaching it is, how pervasive of past and present, how it has formed and defined and will continue to shape the planet and is present in each breath we take. But both these poem,s along with 'Four a.m.'

and 'Evening', are statements about what there is to see when we switch off the news bulletin. The news in a pandemic can be dominated by facts and numbers. What we don't know we fear. But the undefined, the surprising and the unmeasured are places to which we should not forbid ourselves entry.

Mystery

The Moon Came Down

The moon came down among the trees
And brought the stars
And brought me to my knees.

'The Moon Came Down' came in unusual fashion. I glimpsed the full moon through an opaque blind that had been lowered to cover three quarters of the window. In a U-shaped gap between blue gum trees, the moon sat. As my eyes adjusted, the stars appeared and filled the space, then spilled over the treetops and glistened through the foliage. I bent down to get a clearer view, but that was uncomfortable. I knelt on the floor. The scene literally 'brought me to my knees'. It's true to say my body wrote the poem.

Staying in Touch

It Was As If

I spoke with Seamus Heaney last night.
'I wrote a brace of poems for you.
'The first was written the week you died,
The second for your anniversary three years later,' I told him.

And then, in my mind's eye
I saw a stanza from the first. It read,

The light that is his shadow shines,
Shows new paths, ceises, crossings,
Stepping stones, stairways to
Richer, deeper, greener, inner lands.

It was as if meeting this way was like his meeting
With William Strathearn, a shopkeeper murdered
In cold blood by two RUC men in the Troubles.
In his Station Island poems William's shade appeared
And he and Seamus spoke as man to man,
Ordinary, about this and that, life and death, until
'*…he trembled like a heatwave and faded.*'

A breeze rustled the beech trees' leaves.
He raised his bushy eyebrows, there was the hint of a smile.
He remained where he was. The breeze did not blow him away.

'You've been gone a while now,' I said.
The leaves were trembling, and I, whispering
Spoke to him out of the anniversary poem.

'You taught us as you were taught – that mind is vast.
And you like Dante's Virgil our trusty guide. Our how-to
Man, trowel-lifter, spade-wielder. Your poems your life outlast,
Our hearts renew. Fresh shoots our minds imbue.'

His smile broadened. He knew the ground
He'd ploughed and tilled was sown.
Come spring the barley seeds would sprout.

Side by side we stood,
Watching the greening of the brown earth.
The beech trees' leaves and I are silent now.
'What more can a good man hope for?'

'It Was As If' allows an active connection to the person and the poetry of someone significant who has died. I set the scene – 'I spoke with

Seamus Heaney last night' – and proceed to relate our conversation. I refer to and quote from two other poems I had written for him/to him.

I encourage his visiting shade to remain by talking about one of his poems from Station Island and quote from it when I feared him fading. I talk directly to him and tell him in a whisper how he lives on among us and say, 'Your poems your life outlast, our hearts renew. Fresh shoots our minds imbue.' Silence is found between us, out of which he 'speaks' for the first time – the last line of the poem.

If we have established and laid down strong connections to people who have touched and shaped our lives – directly through their life, or through their art – we need, in difficult times, to reconnect.

Mapping Past and Present

What I Do

Some rush headlong. Some stand and wait. Some kneel
And reach under the surface of the great reservoir,
And slowly, moved first by instinct, then by music
And by mind, lift up their hands, liquid full, overflowing.

Practicing my art, my craft, that is what I do.
Then I pour a liquid mirror and offer it to you. I trust
My thoughts and words, your heart and mind, align.
I hope my hands will rise with water turned to wine.

Cartography

How did I come here? How did I find a way?
Those clean and finely-contoured maps
I followed in the morning, faded under midday suns.

Much of what and where and who I visited
Was unexpected. That man I saw ahead not he
Who I've become. Midway, I made my dreams my barge

And found myself on shores of inner worlds,
With silence, science and poems my guides.
Making marks upon time's sands, (like Birnam Wood)

The impenetrable wilderness has come to me.
The beauty of images is found in front of things;
The beauty of ideas, behind. Moon replaces sun.

Life

He thought he'd get through
Being one man.
He came to know,
He'd need to find,
The strength of twenty.

That poems do not draw attention to complex philosophical ideas and abstract truths does not mean that they are absent or non-existent. They may be hidden within the structure in the way steel reinforcements of a high-rise can be hidden within concrete. In the poem, they will be visible only as shadows.

Looking back over my shoulder at 'A Compass Line' and 'Tracing Shadows', it will be in such territory as a compass line and a shadow intersect that we will sense and maybe perceive the presence of the mental activity that produces complex and abstract ideas. 'The beauty of images is found in front of things; / The beauty of ideas, behind.'

Some poems are like the wake a craft makes as it moves across a still lake. Movement at its peaceful best. No words, thoughts, images, sentiments impede or influence its passage. 'What I Do' began as a poem about the art and craft of poem making. Soon it was also about the art and craft of Freud's talking cure, the conversation that is psychoanalysis. They intermingled and became one.

In the early part of the book, I referred to a poem that was complete at its first appearance. Born whole. 'Life' is that poem. As I indicated, I had set about extending it, expecting it to say more, regarding it as the kernel of a longer piece. But the parts I added kept falling off. It was only when I resisted my restlessness and looked at it for what it was that I saw it complete.

On reflection, my best explanation as to why I didn't leave what I had first created alone was that it frightened me. It was like seeing an X-ray or an MRI scan of your brain. Or those moments people who think they are about to die experience, and their whole life appears in a flash. The poem is an echo of 'Cartography', in five short lines, twenty words. A life, my life (and yours?) condensed. When the map that had been written for your life and the one you wrote fail on the edge of a wilderness, and when the impossible and utterly unexpected happens, as when in *Macbeth* Birnam Wood came to Dunsinane, strength like you never imagined existing has to be found.

Reading

Reading

Those dreams, those unbordered visions
You witness, from your eyes I see

Are grammar-less, evade prose-ordered
Words, defy transmission.

Is it birth throes, the pain of thoughts
Unborn that makes your body tremble?

Is your time's end and its beginning
Spinning like a binary star?

Do you hover in clouds and storms
Above the Sirens' songs?

Was that you behind me as I watched
This morning's sunlight paint the ocean white?

Look. Can you see that invisible breeze
Make music among the dancing leaves?

Could our words and thoughts like
Gravity bind all the things we see?

Your Still Life face I read.
Now you are reading mine.

Victoria and Archer

At the corner of Victoria and Archer on a cold Friday night, while everyone is going about the weekend business of winding time down, he is winding it up. He holds the Bible and as people bunch awaiting the change of lights, his voice rises to proclaim the good news of saints for sinners. He reads the words of prophets, speaks of eternal life and calls for repentance.
In a small café, while perusing the menu, in a moment's fantasy I am standing at the opposite corner of Victoria and Archer. I say, 'This planet is our Eden, our fault refusal to eat from the tree of knowledge, our sin to fail to care.'
On our way back he is still reading and talking. In his hands he holds a thousand years of words, stories and poems, an exuberance of minds and imaginations. While waiting for the lights to change I fault my fantasy, my competitive urge. I believe the mystery of Life is beyond us and embrace the liberation that a finite life can give. I have no need to shout it loud.
The lines of ancient words make delicate strands, and, I believe, in the literature of all peoples, should you seek, you will find their soul. I move on. His voice wanes. I wonder if somewhere deep inside he knows he is a lucky man. As he leans into everlasting life does he pause to privilege those silent ones from far away? Does he look back to see those men and women without whose lives and thoughts and words he would not be standing, retelling old stories, reciting old poems on a cold Friday night in Chatswood at the corner of Victoria and Archer?

A certain contrast here. 'Victoria & Archer', a prose poem that tells a very short story, and 'Reading', with its unspoken communication between two people, with no answers and lots of questions posed. Or a series of visions? Preaching and proclamation are redundant in poetry. Poetry is verbal art.

5
Loving Words

I have described how I make these things called poems. I have shown you a number of poems I have made over the years and described what went in to their making. The remainder of the book is a collection of mini essays on poetry itself. In writing these essays, I constructed them like poems in one respect: they leave lots of space for you to do your own imagining and thinking.

Poem making is the most democratic of arts. Presidents and paupers are poets. You can make a poem in your imagination and memory. You don't even need to write it down, if you can't afford the materials of writing. I like that universality. And that you can pick up, in a second-hand bookshop, for the price of a cup of coffee, not one, but a whole collection of masterpieces.

There are poets in every country. They come from all backgrounds, write in different ways, read different books, speak different languages, live different lives. But what they all have in common is a love of words. Words, what can be done with them must touch the heart and incite the imagination of anyone who becomes a poet.

To explore our own unique story with words is a profitable exercise. I will now give part of my story with words. It describes the part played by two languages, neither of which I learned to speak with any fluency, but which have played and continue to play their part in my respect for and love of words.

What took up residence in me and became interwoven with poetic sound, although I didn't think of it as poetry, was the Latin of the Catholic Mass. The seven-year-old altar boy is taught to recite the appropriate responses to the priest, without knowing the meaning of what he says, and is unaware he recites poetry. To the first words spoken by the priest, *Et Introibo ad altare Dei*, he responds, *Ad Deus qui letificat juventutem meam*. 'And I will go onto the altar of God.' 'To the God who gives joy to my youth.' The opening lines of poem/psalm 43. Mass was not simply a religious ritual; also an entry into 1,000 years of the literature that is the Bible.

Until 1962, all the Mass was in Latin, a practice established 1,500 years earlier making it a portal through which the magic and the mystery of transformation was enacted. Small Irish country chapels rarely surpassed the dull and drab when their aesthetics were evaluated, but of an evening as the light dimmed, that didn't seem to matter and sitting alone in the stillness – the small red sacramental light in front of the tabernacle infusing the space with a supernatural presence – a child could experience a peace, an acceptance, a sense of the eternal, which, although he had neither thought nor word to know and express, was, at the same time a transposition to a future Eden and a recreation of times past when, at his mother's breast and in her eyes he perceived eternity.

In *Remembrance of Things Past*, Proust recalled attending the month of May devotions, how hawthorn blossom was used to decorate the church and taking part in what was 'a joyful celebration and a solemn mystery'.

I studied Latin through secondary school without much enjoyment. I have retained some useful knowledge about the etymology of words, given the large amount of English that derives from Latin. I 'inherited' some unhelpful, even harmful influences from a Catholic childhood, but somehow, for reasons not clear to me at present, the beauty of those melodies within the words of the mass have 'survived' within my mind.

*

In Ireland, a schoolchild in the 50s and 60s approaching Gaelic, his native tongue, was served up a complex menu. From infant class to the Leaving Cert, there was no escaping. There were lessons in reading and writing and a failure in the subject at the Leaving Cert meant you failed everything. A fistful of honours in other subjects meant nothing when you applied to university, and a job in the civil service required fluency in the language. Although there were, I was told, everyday fluent speakers in a few parts of the country, I never met one and during all my educational years never heard two teachers have a conversation in Gaelic. In the late 60s, the government, realising the stick, at least that one, was useless, produced the carrot: no longer would you fail in everything if you failed Gaelic; instead an honour in the subject now counted as two.

We had, from the cradle, to also battle history. Gaelic had been in decline since the 1820 or thereabouts. As a true colonising power, British dominance cast a net over the language. Ireland was meticulously surveyed and mapped, all Gaelic place names translated into English. As in Australia, this colonising tool took a wrecking ball to local stories and affiliations, language and history and attachment to place smashed in the one go. My home town, for example, the place where my parents were born and grew up and where I went to secondary school in Country Kildare, was called Athy. The town sits on two sides of a river. Its Gaelic name is Baile Atha Hi, roughly translated as 'the town at the Ford of Hugh'. That leads you back into history to find out who Hugh was. Such knowledge was in or on the edge of people's minds. Athy has nothing to evoke all that, which was of course the point. An efficient coloniser knows the power of a latent memory and history and works assiduously to redact it.

However, from my very impoverished schoolboy perspective, the long and the short of it was that I hated having to learn that dead and that dying language. In my Leaving Cert, I took a pass course in Gaelic. But despite my conscious efforts, something from both languages disappeared inside me. And reappeared when I began to write poetry in my mid-50s.

Latin represented itself in a straightforward manner. While searching for words to capture the silent and sublime, I was transported back in time to the chapel in Barrowhouse. The music of the language had greater longevity than the meaning and I was wordlessly willing to accept transportation.

When Gaelic returned, I was sent into a spin. I wrote a novel called *Boat People*, within which I quoted some words from a Gaelic poem. They were *Go n-éirí an bóthar leat?/ Go raibh an ghaoth go brách ag do chúl*, which translate as 'May the road rise to meet you / May the wind be always at your back.' I had written those words into the text of the novel and silently read them many times through various drafts to galley proofs and finally as printed book. But it was not until I was preparing my thoughts for a book launch that I spoke them aloud in Gaelic. Halfway through the second line. I was overcome by the sound of the word *ghaoth*.

Speaking and hearing myself say the word *ghaoth* after forty years of silence caused me to weep. *Ghaoth* means wind; *an ghaoth*, the wind. It is spelt *g h a o t h*. In Gaelic, 'h' after a letter softens it. The Gaelic alphabet has eighteen letters. There is no English 'th' sound (as in 'those' or 'this') in Gaelic. So the 'g' and 'th' are softened: *ghaoth*. It is pronounced *g'way*. The word onomatopoeic; the sound of a passing breeze. (Say it almost as a whisper.) I tripped over *ghaoth* and I was undone.

Emotionally powered words don't become extinct. They become unconscious. They hibernate. They are carried inside individuals and in communities. It is probable that many emotionally powered words are laid down within us when we are children, particularly when we can hear but have not yet learned to speak. When we meet them again, we have to sound them, to hear them, to know them. I carried these sentiments into another poem which said,

> Lost words lost worlds one and the same
> languages like tall trees drive roots
> deep into the soil of the mind.

6
Beginnings

Going further out from the immediate task of writing, beyond the activities of the mind during composition, there are forces like gravity that work silently within. We become the writer we are, indeed the person we are, because of those forces. Everyone who writes poetry will have a list of such people and the older we get, the longer the list becomes. These forces can be a book, an idea, a specific person, the common features being an awareness of creativity and all that goes with finding it, and, once found, nourishing it and knowing what is needed to sustain it.

A person may begin to write poems by accident or by inspiration. They may have some success but if they are to continue and to develop, there is a lot of work to be done. We see more when we use a broader lens, when we enlarge our minds. Such enlargement is not simply a cerebral activity; it is actions of the emotions and the imagination. Just as a more comprehensive understanding of oneself is an important part of living a humanly creative life, so also a more comprehensive understanding of oneself as a poet fosters poetic creativity and enriches one's poetry.

Enrichment of an individual in any pursuit comes about because of and with others. The study of other writers' minds is a great source of learning and often of encouragement (as when it becomes clear what were their challenges are ours also).

A vast amount has been written about the subject. I have chosen a few poets who highlight what to me are significant issues. My aim is not to be comprehensive, rather to point to the importance of this area should you wish to further advance an interest. I look at three poets (Emily Dickinson, Louise Glück, John Keats) who in the early stage of their writing life were attentive to the conditions that were required to enable them to begin to write and to continue writing.

*

It is in some quarters seen as desirable to read all the books in the Western Canon, the achievement presented as reaching the pinnacle of learning. This aspiration is admirable but inadequate and misguided, and, strangely, positively dangerous. Inadequate because it ignores other canons, an Eastern Canon for example; misguided because it is an impossibility, unless perhaps you did nothing but read all day every day and lived to be as old as Methuselah, who it is said lived to be 969. The positively dangerous element derives from the attitude towards knowledge and learning inherent in the belief.

Psychoanalyst Eric Erickson cast his critical eye over various ways of reading and said,

> Some grasp at knowledge as avidly as the cartoonist's goat who was asked by another whether she had eaten a good book lately; others take their knowledge into a corner and chew on it as on a bone; again, others transform themselves into storehouses of information with no hope of ever digesting it all; some prefer to elude and spread information which is neither digested nor digestible; and intellectual rapists insist on making their points by piercing the defences of unreceptive listeners.

It is a profitable exercise to lower your eyes from the endless volumes in the canons and sit at an empty table. Place on it, in reality or in imagination. the books that have taught you to write (if you are a writer) and the books from which you have learned to think. That is what I do in this section and write about people who have influenced me as a writer. It is a short list and selects a few prominent people. I aim to give a taste of how they use words and open a small window into their minds.

You may know some, all or none of them. That is of secondary importance here because the primary task is with you. And that task involves you lowering your eyes and placing on your table those writers and thinkers that have spoken, do speak, to you, who have shaped your mind, guided your pen and, as your hand moves across the page (or touches a keyboard), whisper silent encouragement.

To be fair to the dead and create a level playing field, don't be misled by thinking you can 'know' a writer by attending their literary function. Even if you avail of an opportunity to talk personally with them, the long-dead scribes may prove to be more generous, more revealing, more willing to share with you the inner workings of their own minds.

And to level the playing field fairly, we should attend to the thousands of new words that have been generated in recent decades, many of which were made to name and communicate the changes of the technological age. They inform, but can also clutter the ear and eye, making a noisy blur when we reach for books from generations and traditions past.

*

Emily Dickinson

In Amhurst, Massachusetts, USA, April 1862, Emily Dickinson wrote to Thomas Higginson, editor of a literary magazine, *The Atlantic*. She sent him five poems and this letter.

> Are you too deeply occupied to say if my verse is alive?
> The mind is so near itself it cannot see distinctly, and I have none to ask.
> Should you think it breathed, and had you leisure to tell me, I should feel quick gratitude.
> If I make a mistake, that you dared to tell me would give me sincere honour toward you.
> I enclose my name, asking you, if you please, sir, to tell me what is true.
> That you will not betray me it is needless to ask, since honour is its own pawn.

When Higginson replied, he suggested she 'tidy' her poetry. Should we tidy her letter? Who and what do we listen to? To a woman who, although she had a group of friends with whom she shared her poems, was making a huge step into a new world. Her mind, she says, is so near itself it cannot see distinctly. It is as if her poetry is like a living presence inside her. Emily Dickinson was born the year William Hazlitt died. I don't know if she knew of him in 1862 or ever got to know of him, but her sentiments in this letter echo his when he said, poetry

> is not a branch of authorship: it is the stuff of which our life is made. The rest is mere oblivion, a dead letter: for all that is worth remembering in life is the poetry of it.

A copy of one of Hazlitt's books is listed in the Dickinson family library catalogue.

In his reply, Higginson asked her about family, friends and her education. She wrote back with more poems.

> Thank you for the surgery; it was not so painful as I supposed. I bring you others, as you ask, though they might not differ. While my thought is undressed, I can make the distinction; but when I put them in the gown, they look alike and numb.
>
> You asked how old I was? I made no verse, but one or two, until this winter, sir.
>
> You inquire my books. For poets, I have Keats, and Mr and Mrs Browning. For prose, Mr Ruskin, Sir Thomas Browne, and the Revelations. I went to school, but in your manner of the phrase had no education. When a little girl, I had a friend who taught me immortality; but ventured too near, himself, he never returned.
>
> You ask of my companions. Hills, sir, and the sundown, and a dog large as myself, that my father bought me. They are better than beings because they know, but do not tell; and the noise in the pool at noon excels my piano.
>
> I have a brother and sister; my mother does not care for thought; and father, too busy with his briefs to notice what we do. He buys me many books, but begs be not to read them, because he fears they joggle my mind. They are religious except me, and address an eclipse, every morning, whom they call their 'Father'.
>
> But I fear my story fatigues you. I would like to learn. Could you tell me how to grow, or is it unconveyed, like melody or witchcraft?

> Two editors of journals came to my father's house this winter, and asked me for my mind, and when I asked them 'why' they said I was penurious, and they would use it for the world.
> I could not weigh myself, myself. My size felt small to me.

This second letter has the same directness that was evident in the first. Her personality reveals itself. Her thoughts, she tells us, come undressed, 'but when I put them in the gown they look alike and numb'. Such language presages what awaits us as we read on. 'When a little girl, I had a friend who taught me immortality; but ventured too near, himself, he never returned', a sentence which lets us know she will attend to the sacred subjects, like immortality, but one that is pregnant with mystery and intrigue. Who is this friend who is so important to her? What happened to him in his ventures? Animals, like her dog, 'are better than beings because they know, but do not tell'. Do we need perhaps to be her 'dog companion' if we are to tune in to the essence of her poems, to listen to her unique voice. Do we have to allow our mind to be joggled? If we wish our mind to grow, are we ready to be touched by melody? And witchcraft? 'I could not weigh myself, myself', is one of those intoxicating assemblages of words which, if we repeat it to ourselves many times, we will be tuning our ear to what we are about to listen to.

A temptation to 'tidy' her is understandable. Our brain can be inclined to fit her in with other poetic styles. But her unusual features – not giving titles to her poems and using frequent dashes instead of punctuation – is not a sign of eccentricity. I need to listen to her like I listen to no other. Sometimes, she hurts the brain. She presents the unexpected right in front of my eyes, in one line, and while I look at it, I become aware there is something going on behind me that beckons for attention. This woman who never published a book wrote 1,778 poems and is now regarded her as one of the greatest poets in the English language is worth listening to.

*

Louise Glück

In October 2020 (the year Covid-19 etched fear and confusion on the mind of the world), poetry found a new voice – clear and fearless – on the world stage, when Louise Glück was awarded the Nobel Prize for Literature by the Swedish Academy, whose spokesman said, 'her poetry honoured the intimate, private voice, which public utterance can sometimes augment or extend, but never replace'.

Glück's poetry has an austere beauty while her prose displays a razor-sharp mind, her essays (few in number) are compact with searing perception and comprehensive insight and repay hours of contemplation and frequent return.

But it was not always so and her story about her childhood and how she learned to think and found freedom to write is most instructive. She has told it herself in an essay called 'Education of the Poet'.

> At 16…I realised, logically, that to be 85, then 80, then 75 pounds was to be thin; I understood that at some point I was going to die… One day I told my parents I thought I should see a psychoanalyst. I had no idea where the idea, the word came from… I was immensely fortunate in the analyst my parents found. My seven-year analysis taught me to think…taught me to use doubt…it gave me an intellectual task capable of transforming paralysis into insight. It is fortunate that that discipline gave me a place to use my mind, because my emotional condition, my extreme rigidity of behaviour and frantic dependence on ritual, made other forms of education impossible.

Describing her psychoanalysis, Louise Glück said,

> [In my analysis] I was learning to use native detachment to make contact with myself, which is the point, I suppose, of dream analysis: what's utilised are objective images. I cultivated a capacity to study images and patterns of speech, to see, as objectively as possible, what ideas they embodied. Insofar as I was, obviously, the source of those dreams, those images, I could infer these ideas were mine, the embodied conflicts mine. The longer I withheld conclusion, the more I saw.

Glück served for a year as the American poet laureate and it was said she was the only person who held the position who did not allow her writing patterns to be interrupted. When she gave her acceptance speech on receiving the Nobel Prize, she talked of the poets who had influenced the way she wrote and what she wrote about.

> I was drawn to the solitary human voice, raised in lament or longing. And the poets I returned to as I grew older were the poets in whose work I played, as the elected listener, a crucial role. Intimate, seductive, often furtive or clandestine. Not stadium poets. Not poets talking to themselves. I liked this pact, I liked the sense that what the poem spoke was essential and also private, the message received by the priest or the analyst.

'The true', she wrote,

> has about it an air of mystery or inexplicability. This mystery is an attribute of the elemental: art of the kind [is] the furthest concentration or reduction or clarification of its substance; it cannot be further refined without being changed in its nature. It is essence, ore, wholly unique, and therefore comparable to nothing. No "it" will have existed before; what will have existed are other instances of like authenticity. The true, in poetry, is felt as insight. It is very rare, but beside it other poems seem merely intelligent comment.

Elsewhere she wrote,

> As a reader, consequently as a writer, I am partial to most forms of voluntary silence. I love what is implicit or present in outline, that which summons (as opposed to imposes) thought. I love white space, love the telling omission, love lacunae...

7
The Enchanter's Cell

William Hazlitt's name has popped up many times and I have encouraged you to listen to him, even if you didn't know who he was. His writing had a profound effect on me becoming a poet. I introduce you to him now, but first let me tell you how I was introduced to him. His writing apprenticeship is an interesting one. He had much to say about the poetic mind and what was needed to nourish a thinking and writing mind.

In 1996 in Sydney, I was a speaker at a conference and my subject was the place of imagination and creativity within psychoanalysis. It was my good fortune to have as a discussant Jane Adamson from the Australian National University. She presented a journey through the last five hundred years of English literature, outlining how great writers had thought about the place of imagination in their creative activity. She referred to William Hazlitt and quoted the following piece he had written when comparing Chaucer's mind and Shakespeare's mind.

> Chaucer had a great variety of powers but he could only do one thing at once. He set himself to work on a particular subject. His ideas were kept separate, labelled, ticketed and parcelled out in a set form, in pews and compartments by themselves. They did not play into one another's hands, they do not react upon one another as the blower's breath moulds the yielding glass. There is something hard and dry in them. What is the most wonderful thing in Shakespeare's faculties is their excessive sociability, and how they gossiped and compared notes together.

I was captivated by Hazlitt's language and wanted to hear more. Seven years later, I had read about a dozen biographies, numerous commentaries, everything he wrote (which stretched to twenty-two volumes) and in 2003 my own book, *Thoughts for the 21st Century: In The*

Company of William Hazlitt, was published by Australian Scholarly Publishing.

In *My First Acquaintance with Poets*, Hazlitt described the events of 1798 that had a profound effect on his life. Samuel Taylor Coleridge, then aged twenty-five, went to Shrewsbury to preach. Hazlitt woke before dawn on a raw, cold, comfortless Sunday and walked the ten miles through the January mud from his home in Wem. The marvellous cocktail of religion, poetry, philosophy and spirituality delivered with great energy and conviction dazzled the nineteen-year-old Hazlitt. Coleridge's voice was like a siren's song that stunned and startled the younger man. 'The light of his genius shone in my soul' was how he described the experience. Before meeting Coleridge, Hazlitt knew that he had a mind capable of profound thought. He also intuitively believed in the value of his ideas. He lacked the faith to express them. Coleridge helped Hazlitt to believe that he would find the proper means of expression.

Later in the same year, Hazlitt visited Coleridge at his home at Nether Stowey, Somerset, and Coleridge took him to meet William Wordsworth, who lived a few miles away at Alfoxden. During the three weeks Hazlitt spent in Wordsworth's company, he was convinced that he had met the most creative and innovative poet of his generation. Wordsworth could take ordinary things in nature and from them create extraordinary poetry. Hazlitt wrote,

> he gathers manna in the wilderness, he strikes the barren rock for the gushing moisture. He elevates the mean by the strength of his own aspirations; he clothes the naked with beauty and grandeur from the stores of his own recollections.

If 1798 had begun and ended in dramatic fashion for Hazlitt, the following year would open on no less profound a note. In the spring, he visited an exhibition of old Italian masters at Pall Mall in London. There began his lifelong love of art and first steps towards becoming a renowned art critic. Hazlitt was in awe of timeless paintings that hung on the gallery walls.

> I was staggered when I saw the works there collected, and looked at them with wondering and with longing eyes. A mist passed away from my sight: the scales fell off. A new sense came upon me, a new heaven and a new earth stood before me. We had heard the names of Titian, Raphael, Guido, Domenichino, the Caracci – but to see them face to face, to be in the same room with their deathless productions, was like breaking some mighty spell – was almost an effect of necromancy! From that time I lived in a world of pictures. Battles, sieges, speeches in parliament seemed mere idle noise and fury, 'signifying nothing,' compared with these mighty works and dreaded names that spoke to me in the eternal silence of thought.

He was commissioned to make copies of some of the great masters at the Louvre and in 1802, during a period of peace between France and England, he went to Paris. On his return to England, he managed to make a meagre living as an itinerant portrait painter. In 1805, his first publication appeared, a book on philosophy called *An Essay on the Principles of Human Action*. He began writing on social policy, wrote a book on grammar, lectured on philosophy, got his first job as a parliamentary reporter with the *Morning Chronicle*. He gave up hope of being a good enough painter. His writing and critical career began to expand with work for the *Champion,* the *Examiner* and the *Edinburgh Review*. By 1817, he was a major essayist, art and drama critic, and political commentator. He died in 1830.

When he relinquished his canvas and brush, Hazlitt painted portraits of people with words. These two portraits, the first of Joseph Fawcett and the second of James Northcote allow us entry into the company Hazlitt kept, the type of person he needed to sustain him as thinker and writer.

> I have heard [Fawcett] explain 'That is the most delicious feeling of all, to like what is excellent, no matter whose it is'. In this respect he practised what he preached... There was no flaw or mist in the clear mirror of his mind. He was as open to impressions as he was strenuous in maintaining them. He did not care a rush whether a writer was old or new, in prose or in verse – 'what he wanted' he

said 'was something to make him think'... He gave a cordial welcome to all sorts, provided they were the best in their kind. He was not fond of counterfeits or duplicates. His own style was laboured and artificial to a fault, while his character was frank and ingenuous in the extreme... Men who have fewer native resources, and are obliged to apply oftener to the general stock, acquire by habit a greater aptitude in appreciating what they owe to others. Their taste is not made a sacrifice to their egotism and vanity, and they enrich the soil of their minds with continual accessions of borrowed strength and beauty.

Fawcett was a Unitarian minister and had a chapel in East London. Hazlitt's final book was called *Conversations with Northcote*. This is a description of a visit to Northcote's painting studio.

His eye is ever open, and reflects the universe: his silver accents, beautiful, venerable as his silver hairs, but not scanted, flow as a river. I never ate or drank in his house; nor do I know or care how the flies or spiders fare in it, or whether a mouse can get a living. But I know that I can get there what I can get nowhere else – a welcome, as if one was expected to drop in just at that moment, a total absence of all respect of persons and of airs of self-consequence, endless topics of discourse, refined thoughts, made more striking by ease and simplicity of manner – the husk, the shell of humanity is left at the door, and the spirit, mellowed by time, resides within! All you have to do is sit and listen; and it is like hearing one of Titian's faces speak. To think of worldly matters is a profanation, like that of the money-changers in the Temple; or it is to regard the bread and wine of the Sacrament with carnal eyes. We enter the enchanter's cell, and converse with the divine presence

8
Poems as Dreams and Dreams as Poems

Connections between poems and dreams can be explored from many perspectives. When I dream during or after writing a poem, I look out for connections, something I haven't thought through enough, not described properly, or too much. I have written a number of poems about dreaming. You can listen to a poem as you would look at a dream. Of course, inner and outer worlds are inconceivable without each other. I try to simply slow a process of interaction down in order to see fundamental elements more clearly.

Poetry has the ability to compress. Read a great poem many times and each time something new is revealed. The poet has compressed words and images.

In creating a poem, a poet can recreate a dream; the form of the poem is a structure parallel to the form of a dream. The features of dreams as described by Freud – displacement, condensation, symbolisation – are features of the poem. What distinguishes the poem maker from the dream maker? Words. In dreams, spoken words are sparse. In poems, they are plentiful.

Some poems are transcriptions of dream images; are conversions of the visual into the literary. As the visual forms of dreams vary, from the simple and coherent to the complex and the incoherent, when numerous scenes overlap and intermingle, so poems in their form vary to reflect such multiplicity. We listen without concern to a solo violin, a quartet, an orchestra and choir and do not call it strange. Why would we call a dream of multiple and contrasting images, or the poem that captures such multiplicity in words, strange?

The poet compresses words and images. It is a common occurrence for a reader to 'know' what a new poem means and yet be unable to 'explain' it. It has reached deep inside where those words and images are compressed, or where words have never been born. (Remember Heaney above.) In dreams, so much is shown in silence. In some poems, I try to replicate the transitional space between speech and silence, to allow the readers to enter those spaces within themselves. 'There is a method of trying periods on the ear, or weighing them with the scales of the breath, without any articulate sound. Authors, as they write, may be said to "hear a sound so fine, there's nothing lives 'twixt it and silence",' William Hazlitt said, quoting James Sheridan Knowles. Or as Tagore said, 'Let not my thanks to thee / rob my silence of its fuller homage.'

9
Ars Poetica

Why are poems written about poems? I expect the reasons to be many. I have done it from time to time and doing so fulfilled a purpose before the purpose could be articulated.

A few provisional statements. It is a reminder that a poem is a made-up thing, a construction that requires art and craft. Opening the back of a mechanical clock, you see all its moving, working parts. These poems can open the back of the poet's mind, how he thinks and what sustains his mind. If you abuse language, you abuse thought. Placing poem-making on show is a statement about the thought and care that words and language require and deserve.

Three poems in this collection here can be placed under the present heading.

'What I Do' is about being a poet and a psychoanalyst, so in equal measure about two things. This allows a reader to look at them side by side. In my book *Thought: The Invisible Essence*, I wrote about the talking cure and the writing cure. 'What I Do' condensed all my prose statements into eight lines.

'Scattered Images Seeking Form' can be about many experiences, one being the act of collecting diverse images into a poem with a clear structure. 'The Assembly Line' is more obviously about the efforts to construct a poem, but then it provides a launching pad describing a common dilemma when trying to find the words and thoughts for the activity in your mind, the losing and gaining of a means of expression.

10
Might Half-slumbering

Our poesy is as a gum which oozes
From whence 'tis nourished. The fire i'th flint
Shows not till it be struck; our gentle flame
Provokes itself, and like the current flies
Each bound it chafes.

William Shakespeare, *Timon of Athens*

In the preface, I asked if the essence of poetry is definable, or if, it, like other forms of art is forever elusive? I'll begin my answer with William Hazlitt's words. 'Poetry', he said,

> is not a branch of authorship: it is 'the stuff of which our life is made' all that is worth remembering in life, is the poetry of it… Poetry is that fine particle within us, that expands, rarefies, refines, raises our whole being.

What Hazlitt said gathers in something of what I believe poetry to be. I can't explain what I think the essence of poetry is. It doesn't submit to explanation. When explanation is attempted, when it is organised to be offered to the rational mind, it is changed. Exposition becomes transposition.

It's like this. Before cameras could see in the dark, a small nocturnal creature emerging from its burrow could not be photographed without lighting up the scene. The introduction of lighting changed what was being observed. To introduce rational explanation is analogous to introducing lighting. It changes the essence of poetry.

In John Keats's poem 'Sleep and Poetry', we find the lines

> a drainless shower
> Of light is Poesy; 'tis the supreme of power
> 'Tis might half-slumbering on its own right arm.

To me, that final line conveys the essence of poetry. The lighting of rationality is not altering the scene.

Bashō, the inventor of the haiku, said if you want to write about a tree become the tree. I've become beech and birch, eucalypts and angophoras. To write 'I'll Never Look into Your Eyes', I 'became' a terrorist. As a poet, you do all sorts of things to yourself. But in each and every poem, regardless of its subject, that liminal presence must have life. Otherwise, it will fail to reach, to touch, refine, rarefy and expand the life of the reader.

My attempt inspired by Keats, with a nod to his nightingale.

Poesy (from French poésie)

<blockquote>
a drainless shower
Of light is Poesy; 'tis the supreme of power;
'Tis might half-slumbering on its own right arm. – John Keats
</blockquote>

'Tis the echo of departing voice,
Calling, calling, calling...
The faint fabric of the final word
A birth song.
New life enshrined
Within the private chambers of the mind.

*

John Keats's idea of negative capability is well known. Also known his replacement of the belief that the human soul is of divine creation, inserted into man. He saw the soul as a potential. The creation of each human soul is a lifelong task, part, though by no means all, of which being the creation and care of a mind. I tread carefully upon commentaries on Keats as I am not a Keats scholar or literature scholar, but in 'Sleep and Poetry' I observe the emergence of creative life in John Keats's soul. And this I see in what he says about poetry.

Following the lines of his which I use in my poem, we find the following:

> The very archings of her eyelids charm
> A thousand willing agents to obey,
> And still she governs with the mildest sway.

He is walking around poetry while at the same time taking a step back, coming in close. Here he touches on its allure. It can charm and provoke obedience. But she, poetry, is not to be swayed by adoration. The poet, the poem, the made-up-thing 'governs with the mildest sway'.

A few lines later, poetry provides balm.

We move on through the poem. And then we face the lines, as though we have come out of thicket and stand upon the top of a mountain with wide ranging views.

> What though I am not wealthy in the dower
> Of spinning wisdom; though I do not know
> The shifting of the mighty winds that blow
> Hither and thither all the changing thoughts
> Of man: though no great minist'ring reason sorts
> Out the dark mysteries of human souls
> To clear conceiving – yet there over rolls
> A vast idea before me, and I glean
> Therefrom my liberty: thence too I've seen
> The end and aim of poesy.

As a true child of Shakespeare, however high you go, however vast or distant your eyes can perceive, concern for the common good and the conditions that encourage and enable it, humility, gentleness, friendship are never far away. A return from the heights is a return to an engagement with ordinary life.

> For sweet relief I'll dwell
> On humbler thoughts, and let this strange assay
> Begun in gentleness die so away.
> E'en now all tumult from my bosom fades:
> I turn full hearted to the friendly aids
> That smooth the path of honour; brotherhood,
> And friendliness the nurse of mutual good.

11
An Invisible Hand

Alfred Tennyson's poem 'Morte D'Arthur' tells the story of how King Arthur received his magical sword Excalibur from the maiden in the lake.

> In those old days, one summer noon, an arm
> Rose up from out the bosom of the lake,
> Clothed in white samite, mystic, wonderful,
> Holding the sword – and how I row'd across
> And took it, and have worn it, like a king.

Sixty years ago, as a schoolboy, I first read that poem and learned large sections of it by heart. Then, for decades, I forgot about it, until one day, browsing in a second-hand bookshop, I found an old anthology of English poetry. When I read the first line, the words and the music of the poem flooded back. I could close my eyes and reliably recite a whole page.

The Irish poet Rupert Strong said that the poet picks up a bow and sends an arrow back through the centuries. My experience in the bookshop was of an arrow coming forward from the centuries from the nineteenth to the twenty-first.

Poetry is no respecter of time, or place. That is one of its great strengths. In the summer of 2008, I was in Lane Cove Park in Sydney looking down on the river and when I imagined Tennyson's magic maiden rising from the still waters, I wrote,

Excalibur's Return

It hasn't rained for weeks.
Lane Cove River is like a pond
the unseen sun
peels shadows

from the trees
silken pillars rest
upon the surface of the water.

From such stillness
wonders are born
from water such as this
Tennyson's magic maiden's arm
'clothed in white samite, mystic, wonderful,'
rose with King Arthur's sword Excalibur.

Close your eyes.
See the surface of your soul
part clean and dry
the jewels of your nightfall
the poetry of your dreams
mystic moments of your past
will rise and shine and reach
beyond your half-forgotten days.

 Stillness is one of the most precious qualities in life. In today's world where frenzied communication is god, it is a rare commodity. When you can live with silence and stillness, your words find a hidden key, and everything you hear and speak changes. Stillness isn't a static place where nothing happens. Silence makes room for imagination, inspiration and the capacity to listen. James Joyce said a piano is a coffin of notes that requires a pianist to play it. John McGahern added that a book is a coffin of words that requires a reader to bring it to life. A poem is a piece of art that allows you to take silence and stillness into yourself.

 Stillness is a condition that promotes privacy. Privacy is another precious commodity that in today's world is under rapacious assault. (A metaphor of biblical allusion is appropriate here. Privacy is a pearl of great price that is often traded as worthless.) Fiction – poetry, short stories and the novel – are great defenders of privacy. If the writer has done his work and created that piece of art, he should glide into the shadows and leave the reader free, in the privacy of his own mind, to imagine things that are exclusively his. Good fiction writers are never instructive. They are present, but at an intimately respectful distance. The artist, according to Flaubert, should not appear any more in his work than God in nature: present everywhere, but nowhere visible.

The artist needs to retain a certain childlike innocence, a natural trust that his inner nature will guide him. 'An artist,' according to the English writer Charles Morgan, 'is a child who stares.' Morgan's description of childish wonder is poetry itself.

> Have you ever watched a child, in the full activity of childhood, halt as though an invisible hand had touched his shoulder, and stare? I remember such occasions in my own childhood, and in my manhood also, when a thing seen, which a moment ago was one of many and of no particular significance, has become singular, has separated itself from the stream of consciousness, and has become not an object but a source. What is the child staring at? Not at the flower or the drop of water or the face. The thing seen, which ordinarily halts our observation, has become not a wall but a window. The opaque has become the serene; he is looking through it… An artist is a child who stares, not at the imprisoning walls of life, but outward through the window.

The invisible hand is a visitation. Visitation from outside, from beyond, is a frequent theme in spiritual traditions. We might speculate as to the nature of the visitation, but there would be general agreement on two counts: it is mysterious and it is outside the power of the visited. Insofar as all these poems – in their original inspiration – come from somewhere beyond my control, a poem that is a response to a visitation, might be considered a prayer, a prayer to the universe, or, as Teilhard de Chardin might suggest, a hymn to the universe.

Having a sense of the poetic is like a sixth sense. But that seems an inadequate description. I would be happier with a description that addressed the expansion of our already existing senses, and the way those senses interact, and assist each other. In some of my poems. I try to capture moments of sensual transition, periods – often brief and ephemeral – where one sense gives way to another, where two (or more) senses overlap or where they each refract different aspects of the same reality.

The poet is not some special creature existing in a rarefied sphere. He is part of the blood, sweat, tears and joy of life. Rilke described the place of the poet in his essay 'Concerning the Poet'. Sixteen oarsmen are rowing a boat upstream. The currents are strong; the task demanding. They pull as one, with outstretched arms, rising from their seats, meeting the forces of nature with determination and respect. One of the oarsmen, while continuing to play his part, sings a wordless song. His voice rises and falls. His singing arises out of the work and the strenuous camaraderie and in the listening the whole crew lift their eyes and look beyond. The pandemic has made many lift their eyes to look beyond life. 'In Endings' and 'This Situation', death was faced. But death is only one form of loss. And the capacity to handle loss, in all its numerous manifestations, is one of the most fundamental skills necessary to live a creative life.

Seamus Heaney described a visit to his Aunt Mary, who for many years of his boyhood was an additional mother. When she was old and frail and bedridden, he would enter her room and he would sit in a chair at her bedside. 'Not much being said or needing to be said.' A mixture of *lacrimae rerum* and *Deo gratias*. An appreciation of the tears that are in the world and gratitude for the gift of life.

For another review of a death experience from which significant things were learned, we can go back to a piece published in *The Tatler* in Dublin, 6 June 1710. Richard Steel looked back to the day his father died when he was a five. His mother, herself smitten with grief,

> …catched me in her arms, and transported beyond all patience of the silent grief she was before in, almost smothered me in her embraces; and told me in a flood of tears, 'Papa could not hear me, and would play with me no more, for they were going to put him under ground, whence he could never come to us again.' She was a very beautiful woman, of a noble spirit, and there was a dignity

in her grief amidst all the wildness of her transport; which, methought, struck me with an instinct of sorrow, that, before I was sensible of what it was to grieve, seized my very soul, and has made pity the weakness of my heart ever since. The mind in infancy is, methinks, like the body in embryo; and receives impressions so forcible, that they are as hard to be removed by reason, as any mark with which a child is born is to be taken away by any future application. Hence it is that good-nature in me is no merit; but having been so frequently overwhelmed with her tears before I knew the cause of any affliction, or could draw defences from my own judgement, I imbibed commiseration, remorse, and an unmanly gentleness of mind, which has since ensnared me into ten thousand calamities; and from whence I can reap no advantage, except it be, that in such a humour as I am now in, I can the better indulge myself in the softness of humanity, and enjoy that sweet anxiety that arises from the memory of past afflictions.

*

I have taken you behind the scenes and give you a glimpse of the work that goes into making a poem. As Yeats said in 'Adam's Curse', we must labour to be beautiful. Sometimes, the shortest poems are the longest in composition. They also may require more from you. They are so pared down, so spare and sparse, that if you don't bring a lot to the reading, they can appear meaningless.

To continue on our journey behind the scenes, I would describe what I attempt to do when I write a poem like this: when you look straight ahead – without moving your eyes – what do you see to your right and left? A poem can offer you the opportunity to be aware of what is on the edge of consciousness. That is why the language of poetry is so often suggestive rather than instructive and the images of poetry, instead of informing, provoke.

Poetry can exist outside a poem. Some writers of prose are more poetic than some poets; the language of prose can be as arresting as poetry.

Shakespeare was distressed by the ravages of time and how it destroyed the beauty of the face he loved. In Sonnet 65, he asks how beauty – 'whose action is no stronger than a flower' – defends itself. Like Shakespeare, we can be brought close to despair. There is nothing we can do, 'unless,' as he says, 'this miracle have might / That in black ink my love may still shine bright'.

This miracle is the poem he is writing. It is the poem we are reading. The words of the poem will forever speak the beauty of his love. A poem is no stronger than a flower, and yet, as Shakespeare says in Sonnet 19, 'my love shall in my verse ever live young'.

Creativity takes many forms. It does not always mean finding something new. It can be the re-finding of what has been lost; the rediscovery of what has always been at our side, but we have not slowed to stillness to make room for its presence. As our life progresses, the storehouse of memory is enriched. There are greater opportunities for revisitation, re-alignment and forgiveness.

Part of the joy of writing poetry is its unpredictability. I have described how my poems always start on their own, their end impossible to predict. A novelist may write their final chapter first and work backwards. For me, and I suspect for most poets, that isn't possible. Our alphabetical wonders appear and tantalisingly fade away. If we're lucky, we snare them. Then we imprint the page: black on white.

In 2021, I was again in Lane Cove Park (and have been hundreds of times in intervening years), this time among the trees, and wrote,

Morning light skims

Horizon.
Gum tree trunks
Brighten.

Sandstone rock
At my feet
Last time dull

Glistens.
Life's best comes
Slant.

*

To take a book called *How to Write Poetry in How Many Chapters* to its conclusion is a challenge. The name itself arose by accident. A two-page introduction to poems written during 2020 sparked interest among those who read them and more was asked for. The 'more' became two 'chapters' which began to bulge and extend themselves. After six chapters, a working title came and stayed. So what's to become in the final chapter?

There has been no end towards which I have been writing; summation is neither possible or desirable. Nevertheless, I don't wish to stop leaving a trail of diffusion and vagueness behind. I will therefore turn my attention to that which is essential to keep alive, to value highly and enable to flourish.

In 'In The Beginning', I wrote of the mystery of Life, which includes the mystery of self-consciousness. What a marvellous thing existence is. Existence is everywhere but we humans are blessed with/have been given the gift of self-consciousness. Some other forms of life have transient and/or limited awareness of 'self'. We have it in abundance.

In Greek mythology (always a place to find the fundamentals), Perseus had a problem. He had to slay Medusa but anyone who looked directly at her was turned to stone. His ingenious solution was to use his mirror like a shield within which he could see her reflection and thereby deliver the fatal blow effectively.

If I try to look directly at self-consciousness, my mind, if it doesn't turn to stone, might as well do. So, talking a clue from Perseus, I offer some reflections.

If I kick a stone, I am conscious of crude pain. If I smell a Mexican orchid, I search for words and come up with chocolate vanilla essence. If we are in the same room, neither speaking or looking at each other and you violently hate me or tenderly love me, that sense of things will enter into my consciousness.

Travelling even further within calls up the ephemeral, the incandescent, the opalescent. But I don't plan to leave you wandering in the ether. We need, if not to come back to earth, to return to our mind and say to ourselves what it is to us. As yet, I have not found sufficient new words, and until I do, I borrow the old. They are the best on hand, the best so far I've found and were put together in 1585 by Edward Dyer, and are still to me going strong.

> My mind to me a kingdom is
> Such present joys therein I find
> That it excels all other bliss
> That earth affords or grows by kind.

Although I have written numerous poems about the land of my birth, they were all written in Australia, where I began to write poetry. There was a need to make a physical connection with my new land and writing poems played an important part in doing just that. I have discovered many things through writing. Poems can take you up close to trees and rocks, to the country that is your home, and launch you on a trajectory towards the greatest mysteries that human minds and hearts have contemplated. Even the perplexities of consciousness itself are not beyond a poem's reach. Magritte said, 'The mind loves the unknown. It loves images whose meaning is unknown, since the meaning of the mind itself is unknown.'

*

Where do we go from here? How about some magic? Rough magic or simple magic? For that, I turn to the poet with the largest vision, a vision that extends into what many believe to be the impossible. The poet is William Shakespeare. And the poetry where the magic of his vision is on display is in Act V of his last work, *The Tempest.*

Prospero, whose own failings and mistakes dwell in the shadows of his mind, does not know the way to redemption, the step through forgiveness. His teacher, whom he sometimes treats as a servant and fails to respect, is Ariel. Prospero has directed his old friend Gonzalo and all his companions to be placed under a spell. Ariel describes Gonzalo's predicament.

> Ariel: His tears runs down his beard like winter's drops
> From eaves of reeds. Your charm so strongly works 'em
> That if you now beheld them, your affections
> Would become tender.
> Prospero: Dost thou think so, spirit?
> Ariel: Mine would, sir, were I human.
> Prospero: And mine shall
> Hast thou, which art but air, a touch, a feeling
> Of their afflictions, and shall not myself,
> One of their kind, that relish all as sharply
> Passion as they, be kinder moved than thou art?

Prospero remains central to the remaining action of the play. The words 'and mine shall' do not depict a sudden, simple conversion. Before Prospero speaks the dramatic words,

> But this rough magic
>   I here abjure,

and adds,

> …I'll break my staff,
> Bury it certain fathoms in the earth,
> And deeper than did ever plummet sound
> I'll drown my book,

he lists the magical acts he has performed, including raising people from the dead. This is the first mention of some of these actions. My sense is that he is in the process of recalling the omnipotent fantasies that have had residence in his mind, to relinquish them. He has much more to do, including acknowledging that the hitherto despised and deformed Caliban represents part of him.

The Tempest is a play full of references to sleep and waking, to dreaming and daydreaming, drowsiness, trance, hallucination – various states of consciousness and unconsciousness. There's lots of music and noise; more music than in any other of Shakespeare's plays. As Harold Goddard said, Shakespeare is interested in the relationship between sleep and music – 'between music and the unconscious mind'.

But for a different, simple magic, I turn to Ariel. In his last play, Shakespeare gives us something new. Ariel is unique among the hundreds of characters in Shakespeare's plays. Ariel is hard to pin down. Ariel is not human. Who is he/she/it? In *The Tempest*, Ariel is often an invisible or disguised presence. When the play is staged, the part can be played by a male or female actor.

Prospero has been wronged and is intent on revenge and uses magic to make the tempest to trap his enemies. He can create a storm, but when anything more subtle is required, he calls upon Ariel. Ariel sends people to sleep. He guides them to safety. He makes the music and the dance. And he can improvise – take the initiative. And Ariel's music is the spontaneous overflow of the joy of life.

Prospero's renouncing of his rough magic coincides with the release of Ariel. Wonder in the ordinary replaces the performance of wonders. Ariel achieving freedom is pivotal. Ariel is the agent of internal miracles. Poets wait for Ariel's presence at their side. There is stillness and a quietness about Ariel, a stillness and a quietness that is only to be found in the ordinary and the everyday. Ariel's transition takes place quietly. When Prospero gives up his magic, he goes with a flourish. (In one stage production, his book ignited into flames.) Ariel has already told us where to find him.

> Where the bee sucks, there suck I;
> In a cowslip's bed I lie;
> There I couch when owls do cry;
> On the bat's back I do fly
> After summer merrily.
> Merrily, merrily, shall I live now,
> Under the blossom that hangs on the bough.

The stage play will end with Prospero's Epilogue. But I think of Shakespeare's last play as having two endings, the other – more important one – is when Ariel makes an exit.

A poem is a thing from the real and the imagined. When I write a poem and someone reads it, I am offering them a connection with me in a real and an imagined way. If the reader, or the listener if they hear me, are able to combine those two entities, they can receive something. Henry James said,

> Experience is never limited, and it is never complete; it is an immense sensibility, a kind of huge spider-web of the finest silken threads suspended in the chamber of consciousness, and catching every air-borne particle in its tissue. It is the very atmosphere of the mind; and when the mind is imaginative…it takes to itself the faintest hints of life.

Ariel is the imaginative, inventive spirit of Shakespeare. It's his legacy to us. His great works only become great to us when we receive them with our imaginative, inventive mind. This Ariel, this spirit, this gift, exists quietly, takes to itself the faintest hints of life, works its wonders internally. Its fine magic uses simple words, the words of poetry, which will, no matter how dark the world becomes, continue to shine a light.

See you on the far side of time.
It is not a place.
There are no signposts.
You walk alone.

Trust ancient symbols, sounds
Which pre- and post-date words,
Ambient touch,
Scents that are indescribable,
Visions opalescent,
Crepuscular,
Slender as gossamer,
Offered to the inner eye.

Strands searching for
The spirit of thought,
Must need await
Their braiding.

www.ingramcontent.com/pod-product-compliance
Lightning Source LLC
Chambersburg PA
CBHW050303120526
44590CB00016B/2469